Grace for Eliza

Shannon Schulz

Trilogy Christian Publishers
A Wholly Owned Subsidiary of Trinity Broadcasting Network
2442 Michelle Drive
Tustin, CA 92780

For information, address Trilogy Christian Publishing
Rights Department, 2442 Michelle Drive, Tustin, Ca 92780.
Trilogy Christian Publishing/ TBN and colophon are trademarks of Trinity Broadcasting Network.

For information about special discounts for bulk purchases, please contact Trilogy Christian Publishing.

Manufactured in the United States of America

10 9 8 7 6 5 4 3 2 1

Library of Congress Cataloging-in-Publication Data is available.

ISBN 978-1-64773-752-8 (Print Book)
ISBN 978-1-64773-753-5 (ebook)

For my parents—
you never stopped believing in me.

Contents

Acknowledgments

There are so many people to acknowledge in the writing of this story. First and foremost is our Lord and Savior, Jesus Christ, who forever changed my desires and perspective. Secondly, I thank my other half, Joel. The Lord chose best for me, and I praise Him for your passion to follow Him on the path of righteousness. You have loved and led us well! Thirdly, I thank our parents, who raised us to love and seek the Lord. I also thank our families for being there for us when we needed them. You heard our pleas and came. Lastly, I thank our girls, who have loved us in spite of our parental and personal faults. We've moved you all over this great country, stretching your faith, and you never complained! You have borne well under pressure, and we see the diamond of godliness developing within.

There are more people to thank than I can list here, but please know your loving care for our family is forever imprinted on our hearts. From the nursing staff at Children's Hospital to the incredible doctors we've met, you are our heroes! You spend countless hours caring for your patients, often without recognition, but we've seen you. We've watched you under stress and in the quiet hours of the hospital, fighting on our behalf. Thank you!

To those in the many churches who prayed for us, gave us meals, sat with us in waiting rooms, and encouraged us in our darkest hours, we thank you. The church is an amazing body, designed by the Lord for the purpose of carrying one another's burdens. You carried ours well, and I know the Lord was honored. I thank those who continued to encourage me to put in book format what we lived firsthand. And thank you to my team of readers who gave me welcome feedback. My history, which is His story, has come to life in these pages, and I pray it blesses many to trust Jesus with all their hearts.

I have tried to recreate events, locales, and conversations from my memories of them. In order to maintain their anonymity in some instances, I have changed the names of individuals and places.

All scripture quotations, unless otherwise indicated, are taken from the New International Version.

The Nightmare

Sent: *Tuesday, September 12, 2006, 9:01 a.m.*
Subject: *Our baby in the ICU*

Dear loved ones,

To those near and far, yesterday Joel and I experienced every parent's worst nightmare, the fear of losing a child. I write asking for prayers as our little Eliza Grace is very sick and is currently in the ICU at Children's Hospital.

We may be in for a long road or a short stint— we aren't sure. So please pray with us!

It is believed that this may have started by her being infected by E. coli *that went untreated for so long. We just need to make it through today.*

Love and weariness,
Shannon, for all of us

I stood holding my diaper-clad twenty-three-month-old daughter, trying hard not to disturb the many wires attached to her small frame as our pediatrician's words began to wield their way into my consciousness: "Keep praying, Shannon. *Please* don't stop! I don't know how to tell you this, but Eliza is very sick, and I'm afraid she may not survive the transfer to Children's Hospital." The fervency of her voice combined with the evident fear in her eyes caused my world to come to an abrupt halt. Looking across the small hospital room, I saw Joel

9

slumped over in the bedside chair, slowly running his fingers through his hair, seemingly in a far-off land, navigating his own thoughts. I longed for him to look at me. I willed him in my mind to offer me some source of encouragement, but there was none as he remained frozen in his own world. There was just the eerie, repetitive thumping of Eliza's heart monitor ringing in my consciousness, tying me to the little life she held.

I've known my husband, Joel, since we were young children in Sunday school together. He lived on the opposite side of town, attending different schools, but we remained friends over the years through various church programs, camps, mission trips, and youth group. I clearly remember him pulling my braids more than once in elementary school and crushing on him in junior high with his bright-green crimped pants and red Converse. He was an eighties skateboarder with long bangs and a flare for the dramatic, making him, in my mind, the perfect beau. But as such things go, nothing happened until our high school years, when the Lord clearly told my heart Joel would be a large part of my life someday. There are very few instances in my life where I can *clearly* say the Lord spoke to me, but this was one of them. And my reaction wasn't quite what one would expect: I ran.

Every time Joel showed any interest in getting to know me better, I found ways to push him off. We still laugh today about a time when he asked me out to dinner and I told him we had a planned family night. My good girlfriend called right after him, wanting to hang out for the evening as we gleefully headed downtown, giggling over my ditching of Joel—that is, until I returned home and my sister told me Joel had called twice and was expecting a return phone call. "He wants to know how your family time went. Why did you lie to him?" *Ugh. Do I have to explain myself?*

Joel made me pay for my crime by treating me to ice cream, me wearing a silly straw hat and corsage. We laughed over our banana split as I continued to scheme ways to "get rid of him." Now, understand, it was *not* that I didn't like him—quite the contrary! It was those clear words that kept echoing in my heart, "A large part of your life." As a high school senior, I wasn't ready for anything serious or

Joel's persistence, which unfortunately led to a broken heart. *Fine*, I thought, *my job here is done. If he's really meant for me, then You'll make that clear later. And mend whatever I just broke.* True to His word, the Lord did just that.

As I held my daughter's limp body, my mind swirled. *What do I say?* Each breath could be Eliza's last, and yet I found myself at a profound loss for words. My mind raced with the many things I longed for her to know, and yet the intensity of the moment kept me silent. I held her tighter, as if that would keep her from slipping away from this life. Just as quickly as she entered my world, she could depart. She wasn't mine; she was a gift, a precious gift. Snuggling her close, stroking her wavy blond hair, I whispered quietly in her ear, "Mommy loves you, dear one. We love you. Please know how much we love you. Jesus loves you. You are His. He will meet you—look for Him, love. We will see you there."

Shattering the moment and demanding attention, Zoë, our four-year-old daughter, bounded into the room, gushing with life as she skirted past the crash cart and overlooked the ominous machines surrounding Eliza. She looked to me for answers, and I offered a weak smile through my tears. How I wish she didn't have to see me this way; she was too young to understand. Sensing the weight of the room, Zoë turned and approached Joel. "Daddy, why sad? What's wrong with Eliza?"

As quickly as Zoë entered, a good friend who was one of many scattered up and down the hallway bounded after her to gather her and Eliza's twin sister, Robin, for an overnight "adventure" at their house. Offering smiles of comfort, they quickly departed, leaving an empty space in my heart. I longed to casually walk out of the hospital with the life I knew a few days ago. The sterile hospital walls were falling in on me like a prison, void of all feeling, echoing the lifelessness I felt.

As if reading my thoughts, Eliza moaned in my arms. She was such a beautiful baby. I know all moms believe their babies are the most beautiful creatures to grace God's earth, and they are all right! Each baby is beautiful to their mother as they forever steal their hearts.

Eliza had been graced with an earthly beauty from the day she was born with big baby-doe eyes framed by long black lashes, her wavy blond hair complementing her oval face and high cheekbones. The unassuming humility and grace behind her smile embraced those in her presence. Even after being poked and prodded by the nursing staff, she always had a smile to offer, flowing from the grace in her eyes. Her love for people captivated and drew them to her.

Eliza was vastly different from her twin sister, Robin, who was born with a beauty of her own. Her round face was topped with troll doll hair that whisked when provoked. She was active from inception, always moving and leaving a ripple of laughter behind her crazy antics and sense of humor. Her insatiable curiosity led to many dismantled remote controls and toys as we tried to control our frustrations. Yes, to Robin the world was an open book meant to be simultaneously explored and enjoyed.

My pregnancy with the twins was planned as we figured the timing of two and a half years between our children was about right, but having twins was never an issue Joel and I thought to discuss. Since this was my second pregnancy, I went to the standard nine-week OB visit not expecting anything out of the norm. The nurse requested to check the baby's heartbeat with a Doppler just to ensure everything was progressing normally. I thought it was quite strange when she found a fast heartbeat on the left side of my abdomen but then lost it. Unable to relocate it, she ventured to my right side, where again she located another quick heartbeat. I remember thinking, *Man, that baby moved really quickly for being so little. I didn't know they could do that.* As if pondering the same question, the nurse said, "I'll be right back. I'm going to get Dr. Harris."

The doctor came in confidently. "I think we'll do an ultrasound just to be sure the baby is doing well. I don't think there is anything to be concerned about. I'd just like to check the heartbeat." As she pulled the black-and-white sonogram image up on the screen, she chuckled. "Well, look at that, there's two of them."

"What?" I asked, as if she were speaking a foreign language.

"You are carrying twins. Do you see that? There are two separate heartbeats."

Flustered, I responded more curtly than I intended, "Are you sure? Are you sure that machine is working right? We don't have any twins in our family. I can't possibly be carrying twins."

Chuckling again, Dr. Harris pointed to the screen. "Yes, I'm positive you're having twins. Don't you see that? There are two very distinct heartbeats. And from their distance apart, I'm confident they're fraternal. They're too far apart to have split from each other. You must have released an egg from each ovary, which isn't that uncommon. Here, I'll print out this picture for you to take with you. You can show it to your husband."

My husband! Oh my, what is Joel going to think?

Walking out of the room, Dr. Harris announced to the office staff, "She's having twins!" There was a great deal of "Oohing" and "Aahing" echoing in the distance as the door shut behind her.

Twins? Really, twins? How can this be? Oh, dear.

As I approached the reception desk, the office staff congratulated me and cooed over Zoë in her umbrella stroller. One woman touched my hand. "Are you all right, Shannon? You look a little white. Do you want me to call a ride for you?"

"Uh...no, I need to go to my husband's office. I'm not sure what he's going to say. I'm still in shock. Two...two of them?"

Smiling, she patted my hand. "I'm sure he's going to be thrilled! But perhaps you should sit down for a minute before you go."

"No, I need to go now." Glancing at my watch, I noticed it was his lunch hour. "I need to catch him before his afternoon patients."

Dazed, I drove to the clinic where Joel worked as a prosthetist, Zoë giggling from the back seat. Upon arriving, I approached the reception desk, requesting to see Joel. "Oh, I believe he's still at lunch with Scott and some of the guys."

With disappointment and agitation, I responded, "Oh, do you know when they'll be back? I really need to see him." Thoughtlessly, I began pacing.

Peggy, who was handling the phones over the lunch hour, said, "Hmm, I'm not sure. Probably soon, though. I can call Scott's cell phone to ask." Flustered and unsure, I said I could wait. "Are you sure? Are you all right, Shannon? Is there something I can do for you?"

"Oh, I don't know. I just really need to see Joel. I just found out we're having twins."

"Ahh, that's great news! I'll get Joel on the phone for you! Just hold on!" Picking up the phone, she started dialing. "Hi, Scott, this is Peggy. Is Joel with you? His wife needs to talk to him."

She handed me the phone, and I responded in a daze, "Joel? Where are you? Are you almost back to the office?" (How could I tell him over the phone? I needed to see his reaction; this was too big to tell him this way.)

"Yeah, we're just a few minutes away. Why?"

"I'm in the reception area, waiting to see you. I really need to see you."

"I'll be there in a minute."

He handed the cell phone back to his boss, and Scott asked, "Is everything all right?"

"Yeah, I think. Shannon just got back from her ultrasound and is waiting back at work."

Smiling, Scott asked, "Was she crying?"

"No."

"But she's flustered?"

"Yes, I'd say so."

With a burst of humor, Scott announced, "Dude, I bet you're having twins! My wife was the same way when we found out we were having twins. It's got to be twins. Otherwise, she would be crying!"

Within minutes, a tightly packed group of men bounded to the front desk, surrounding Joel. I looked at him, placing the ultrasound pictures on the desk as I was pushed out by the many onlookers. Before I could say a word, Scott started laughing, slapping Joel on the back. "I told you! You're having twins!" With great excitement, he picked up the intercom and announced to the whole office, "Joel and Shannon are having twins!"

Tears laced the edges of Joel's eyes as he beamed in excitement, happiness, and pride gushing from every feature. He came to me, pulling me in a big embrace, as Zoë giggled and pulled at his pant leg. Looking at him, I asked apprehensively, "So you're happy?"

"Yes! Of course I'm happy! This is great news!" Pulling back and looking at me beseechingly, he asked in earnest, "Aren't you happy?"

"I don't know what to think. I have to carry *two* babies and take care of them. I could barely handle one baby after Zoë's birth. How will I manage two?"

His concern turned to humor as he said confidently, "Oh, Shannon, you'll do great! I just know it!" And with that, tears of joy filled our hearts.

My pregnancy was very normal. I had trouble gaining weight at the beginning, which was concerning with twins, but other than that, everything was very predictable. Once we approached the mid-point, we figured we were entering a time of uncertainty as thoughts of premature labor loomed. But to my own distress, I continued to carry them well into my thirty-eighth week, which is considered full term for twins. I was so uncomfortable I couldn't stand for longer than ten minutes, and sleep was impossible as all three of us fought for space from any given position—sitting, standing, lying down, etc.

Robin, who occupied the left side of my uterus, was in constant motion, which was what inspired her name, as I told Joel, "This one needs to be named Robin since she's flighty like a bird!" Eliza, occupying the right side, was a direct contrast to Robin, always very serene and patient. She was engaged first for delivery, which is why I believe I carried them so long—Eliza had nowhere to go! She was quite comfortable where she was. We used to imagine Robin on the other side constantly kicking Eliza (and me!) to get her to move out of the way since she had a whole new world just waiting to be explored!

At thirty-nine weeks, my OB induced labor on October 5. Eliza was born first, weighing six pounds, ten ounces, and nineteen inches. Robin followed quickly behind seven minutes later, weighing six pounds, six ounces, and eighteen and a half inches long—thirteen pounds combined! It was one of the happiest days of our life as we felt showered in God's blessing and love. We had two beautiful, healthy baby girls, perfect in every way.

Hearing the departing voices in the hospital corridor, I found myself jealous of Zoë's and Robin's naivete, to be able to live as a child free from the burden threatening the world I had carefully crafted. Many questions clouded my thoughts. Would they have a sister come tomorrow morning? How would we explain it to them? Just a week ago, Robin and Eliza had been playing together in their own mischievous way. Although they weren't able to communicate verbally, they had a language of their own, which often led to many crazy antics and torrents of giggles. They were inseparable; although fraternal twins, they had always been considered as one. How would Robin live without Eliza?

Pictures and fragments of conversation from the past week twitched at the edges of my mind. Could seven days really threaten the comfortable life I had known?

Our week had started as any other; as a stay-at-home mom, I had a schedule to keep and errands to run. Joel had been out of town the week prior for work, and we were enjoying his return.

Monday morning, I waited at the prearranged location set by a local farmer to pick up our weekly raw milk supply. Every week I met a woman who was willing to make the hour-and-a-half drive north to pick up the milk directly from the farm, which was required by law. In the state of Oklahoma, you could only buy raw milk directly from the farm. With a car full of antsy children, I waited on the side of a rural road outside of Edmond, Oklahoma, Monday mornings at ten o'clock for Sally.

Raw milk was a new phenomenon in our house. I had a friend who had encouraged me to try it to help with Eliza's allergies and eczema, which were particularly bad that summer and early fall. She would often scratch herself until she bled, making it difficult to offer much physical comfort. I had never heard of raw milk before but figured it was worth trying, like so many of the other lotions and remedies that had been suggested over the past year. I had also been reading about its many health benefits and figured it was worth introducing in our diet, which led me to start making my own butter and whey.

For six weeks, I had been playing with different recipes and uses for raw milk. I was enjoying myself, but my husband, Joel, had other thoughts on the matter. He disliked the taste of raw milk and felt "icky" ever since its introduction to our daily diet. Zoë also missed her ice cream milk, which came from a local dairy chain.

Early Wednesday morning, I was alarmed to find vomit on the floor in Eliza and Robin's room as I peeked in on them. Upon further inspection, Eliza was covered in junk and was obviously not feeling well. Robin seemed a bit down, but not as tired as Eliza. I took their temperatures and was pleased they were only in the low ninety-nines. I figured Eliza must be fighting a mild stomach flu, but wasn't overly concerned. By the end of the day, Zoë and Joel started complaining of an upset stomach, and I realized I was feeling feverish, but none of us had a fever.

Thursday morning, I called Sally to ask her if she had heard of anyone else using raw milk that was complaining of similar symptoms. It dawned on me then that she had her daughter with her at our recent milk exchange and had mentioned she wasn't feeling well.

After I explained our symptoms, Sally's first response was, "No, I haven't heard of anyone else, but I wouldn't tell your doctor that you're using raw milk. In fact, I would avoid seeing them if you can."

"How is your daughter feeling? On Monday, you had mentioned she wasn't feeling well."

"She's fine, and I haven't heard of anyone else." After an awkward silence, our conversation ended, leaving me with a sense of foreboding and suspicion that we were fighting more than just a stomach virus.

With fear lingering at the edges of my consciousness, I picked up the phone again to call my friend who had originally introduced me to raw milk. I explained what was happening to see if she had any insight. Sensing my fear, she offered, "I'd call and ask your doctor if there is something she can do for Eliza without seeing her directly."

I hung up the phone with a strange, sinking feeling as fear threatened to consume me. I did everything I could to push it down, but some questions wouldn't leave me alone: Had I done something wrong? Was raw milk so bad that I shouldn't tell our doctor? What would she do if she did know? I had no idea using raw milk would lead me to this kind of "secrecy." The wisdom of my decision was hanging heavily over me. If I had known it would be this way, would

I have still chosen it as an option? I didn't know what to do, but one thing was for sure: I felt very alone.

Friday morning, Eliza was still nauseous and not eating or drinking well. I decided it was time to call our pediatrician to see if there was something she could do. I did as suggested and didn't mention the raw milk. I also asked if there was a way she could help without seeing Eliza. With a full schedule at hand, she willingly prescribed an antinausea gel that had to be compounded by a local pharmacist, but warned it would make Eliza pretty lethargic and weak.

After picking up the gel and applying it, we drove to our favorite biannual consignment sale to buy the girls winter clothes. Eliza was so tired and weak she slept through most of it in our umbrella stroller. Every now and then, someone would comment on how bad she looked, threatening to undermine any composure I appeared to have. The frightening questions and thoughts that I had done something terribly wrong continued to haunt me, growing stronger with each hour that Eliza showed no sign of improvement. But what had I done wrong?

Saturday morning, I screamed as I was changing Eliza's diaper—there was bright-red blood in her stool. Shaking, I called the on-call doctor at our pediatrician's office. She was rather nonchalant about the whole affair. Right before my call, she had spoken with another mother whose daughter had similar symptoms as Eliza. She reassured me that there was a bad stomach virus going around and figured Eliza had just popped a blood vessel from her consistent diarrhea through the week. She said that if she seemed to get worse, to take her to the ER.

Worse—what constitutes worse? She looks pretty bad now.

I called my parents next, to ask them what they thought. My mom had been a practicing nurse years ago, and my father was a retired dentist, so I figured between the two of them, I would get a second opinion. Fighting the shouting of the CU football game they were attending in Boulder, Colorado, we decided to go with what the doctor had said.

Saturday came and went without Eliza eating or drinking anything. She was very weak and lethargic, but we assumed that was to be expected with the antinausea medication. Since she had stopped vomiting, we figured the medicine was working, although her stools continued to darken in color.

Sunday was a hard day for me. Eliza was growing weaker and weaker, still not eating or drinking anything. In our mind, we didn't know what constituted *worse* from a doctor's perspective. We had never dealt with serious health issues before and were full of uncertainty with taking her to the ER.

After church, we went to a local park to play. Eliza was so weak I had to carry her everywhere. That night, as I was tucking the girls in for bed, I watched Eliza for a while as she tossed and turned in her bed. She was sick, very sick. My mommy intuition was on full alert by this time, and I remember telling Joel, "I have this weird, frightening feeling that Eliza could just drift away from us tonight." With trepidation, he said, "Nah! She's not that sick, is she?" I chose to stay up most of the night, holding her, as I knew sleep would be elusive for both of us.

First thing Monday morning, as the clock struck eight, I immediately called our pediatrician's office. I spoke with the nurse and relayed the past five days to her. She asked me, "When was the last time Eliza had a wet diaper?"

"Uh, probably last Friday, but she hasn't been eating or drinking, so I wasn't expecting her to have wet diapers."

My heart leapt into my throat as she responded, "Hang up the phone right now and take her to the ER immediately. Please don't wait. She should have had a wet diaper even if she wasn't drinking."

Fighting tears, I called a good friend, Connie, who was like a grandmother to us, and asked if she could come over to watch Zoë and Robin. Once I said the word ER, without hesitation she said, "I'll be right over." I put Eliza and the girls on the couch to watch a video as I ran to take a quick shower since I had been up most of the night. When I finished, I didn't see Eliza on the couch. She was lying on her back, staring at the ceiling near our kitchen, which was twenty feet away. She must have crawled there, looking for me, and the hurt of her weakness shattered me into a thousand pieces.

Not knowing where the Children's Hospital was located and hearing many good things about a hospital near us, I drove there as calmly as possible, figuring a hospital is a hospital. I purposely chose not to change Eliza's diaper since I wanted the doctor to see it. Her stools were becoming a darker and darker licorice color, which was far from normal.

By the time we were placed in an examination room, all my energy had been zapped. The immediacy of the moment followed by waiting was exhausting. I was soon greeted by a jovial older doctor who quickly glanced over Eliza's chart. Stopping abruptly, he blurted out, "Your husband works for Scott Sabolich Prosthetics?"

"Yes, he does," I said, wringing my hands, hoping we could turn our attention to Eliza lying engulfed on the hospital bed.

"Man, they are doing some really neat things over there for the prosthetic community. I really admire those guys. Is your husband coming by today?"

"I think so. He should be here soon. I wanted you to take a look at Eliza's diaper."

"Ah, yes. Let's see," he said, returning to her chart and looking over her vitals. "Hmm, well, it looks like she may have a stomach bug. I think we will give her a bolus of IV fluid [which is equivalent to 2.1 cups] and an antibiotic. By the end of the day, she'll be right back to her old self. We'll also draw some labs." And with that, he left, leaving me with many questions but also hopeful Eliza would be herself soon, freeing me from the guilt that was building in my heart.

Two nurses came in to draw labs and start Eliza's IV fluid. I mentioned her diaper again, and after looking at it, they decided to take a sample for the lab. They scraped off what they could, although most of it had been absorbed by the diaper, and placed it in a tube.

After another half-hour, the same nurses started an IV antibiotic. One nurse started looking through the trash when she said, "Oh, well, it looks like housekeeping came through and already took it out." When prodded, she mentioned the lab didn't have enough of Eliza's stool sample to test and requested the whole diaper, which they had thrown in the trash after taking the sample. Oh, well, there wasn't anything that could be done now.

The doctor poked his head back in to check on us and to let us know Eliza would be admitted to the hospital and transferred to an upstairs room for the remainder of the day until her pediatrician could see her. There was no mention of her labs, just a request to the nursing staff to administer a second bolus of fluid before her transfer, since Eliza's CO_2 levels were very low, indicating dehydration, and she still had not peed.

Once we were settled in a private patient room, we spent the afternoon watching the five-year memorial of September 11, 2001, as it was aired on every station available. Another set of labs was drawn, which resulted in a third bolus of fluid, and sadly, still no pee. Throughout the afternoon, Eliza seemed to become more and more uncomfortable, squirming in my arms and unable to lie still. As she began moaning, it was becoming more obvious she was hurting. By 6:00 p.m., Joel called, offering to bring me dinner and the girls for a visit to see Eliza. We had a quick bite to eat before our pediatrician, Dr. Shelli White, arrived to see us. Knowing her from church and running in similar social circles, Joel exchanged a few casual words with her before taking Zoë and Robin to the playroom down the hall.

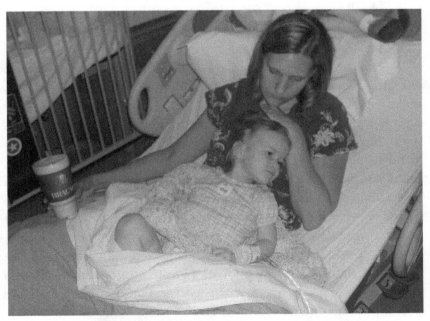

At All Saints Hospital before being seen by Dr. White

Taking out her clipboard and making herself comfortable at the end of Eliza's bed, she asked with concern, "All right, Shannon, I need you to tell me what you can about Eliza." I spent about ten minutes describing what I could remember from the week, shyly ending with, "Shelli, we've been drinking raw milk. What do you think is wrong with her? I'm really getting scared. She seems to be getting worse."

With compassion and exhaustion in her eyes, she replied, "Well, I have a few options to consider. To be honest, her labs don't add up, especially since she's had three bolus of fluid. Her CO_2 levels haven't changed any throughout today, and she still hasn't peed. She could have rotavirus, but I'm not sure, given her labs. Before I say more, I want to make a few phone calls. I have a really scary option and a not-so-scary option, but either way, I believe she will have to be hospitalized for at least a week. I'll be right back after I make these phone calls."

Stepping out of the room, I sought out Joel to give him the news. "How are we going to handle a week with her in the hospital? You have your own patients, and I have the girls to care for. Perhaps I should call my parents. What do you think?"

"Yeah, that probably makes the most sense."

"Joel, I'm scared…"

"I know, but we have to trust the Lord. He's not in heaven wringing His hands. He knows what's wrong with Eliza," he said, pulling me into a warm embrace.

It was only a few moments before Dr. White entered Eliza's room. Sitting down on the bed, she looked at us very seriously. "I'm afraid I don't have very good news. I'm afraid it's the scary option. Eliza's kidneys have stopped functioning. I talked to the on-call nephrologists at Children's Hospital about Eliza's labs, and she confirmed that her kidneys are not functioning, which is why she hasn't peed for three days or after being administered three boluses of fluid. Her CO_2 levels haven't changed either. The nephrologists would like Eliza to be transferred to Children's Hospital as soon as possible to get the care she needs. She is very, very sick. I'm so sorry. I don't have doctor privileges there, so I won't be able to go with you."

Sinking further into my chair, heart racing, I blurted out, "How? How did they stop functioning?" The haunting questions from the past week flooded my mind as I started to shake, battling my composure.

Momentarily holding her breath, as if searching for the right words, she quietly answered, "I'm afraid it may have come from *E. coli.*"

"Which she most likely got from the raw milk, right?"

"Possibly. I don't know what may have caused this for sure, but I do know based on her labs that she needs immediate care."

I felt as if all the blood in my body had rushed into my ears as they began burning. Every cell in my body was on high alert. My heart was beating at marathon speed as my world began to swirl. *Did I do this? Oh, Lord, did I do this? Help me, Lord. The ground of my world is giving out under me.*

Patting my arm, she got up with determined force. "I need to speak with the nurses and get the emergency transfer in motion."

Fighting paralysis, I called my parents, who were three hundred miles away. Given the urgency at the turn of events, my mom said, "We're leaving Denver now. We just need to grab our bags and get on the road. We will get there as soon as we can. We love you, honey. Hang in there. It's going to be all right."

Within minutes, women from our church and my Bible study were filling the hallway outside Eliza's room as Dr. White, who knew them as well, worked feverishly to care for Eliza. She was working the crash cart in place next to Eliza's door when they addressed her. Frantic, she turned to them. "I'm sorry, ladies. I'm really crazy right now. This is a very serious situation that demands my full attention." With that, she swiftly turned into Eliza's room. The women who knew her best could see the fear and worry etched in her body language, which heightened the situation, as Shelli was typically a very easygoing, loving person. The seriousness of the situation struck me again as the tears welled in my eyes.

I hugged the women in the hall as they surrounded me, and walked back into Eliza's room, where I saw her stripped down to her diaper and covered with wires. Cautiously, I asked Dr. White, "May I pick her up?"

"Yes." That was when she relayed to me her fear for Eliza, that she might not survive the transfer to Children's Hospital. "Pray, Shannon, please pray and don't stop. She is very, very sick."

The ambulance EMTs placed their gurney outside Eliza's room as they talked with Dr. White. After five minutes, they walked in to give me instructions. "We originally weren't going to have you ride with us in the ambulance, but seeing how young Eliza is, we'd like you to be with her to help keep her calm. However, she is very sick, and we may have to resuscitate her somewhere on the way if she should crash. Dr. White is concerned she could fall into respiratory arrest, which would require our full attention. If that should happen, we will pull the ambulance over and ask you to get out while we help Eliza. We need your cooperation, that you will stay out of our way and stand on the side of the road while we work. Otherwise, it might be best you not come with us in the ambulance. Are you willing to help us?"

In almost a whisper, I responded, drained of all energy, "Of course, I'll do whatever you need me to. Just please let me stay with her."

"All right, let's get this show on the road. If you will step out of the room, we'll get Eliza settled on the gurney." Looking toward Joel, he offered, "This may take us a while, so why don't you go ahead and meet us at Children's? We'll see you in the ER."

Joel turned to me, trying to offer comfort while reassuring himself. "I'll meet you there. Remember, God knows the number of hairs on her head." He turned to leave, offering a weary smile of assurance. "The Lord has not forgotten us. We have to trust, we have to trust Him."

Leaving the hospital and starting the twenty-minute drive to Children's Hospital, Joel had time to pray and give Eliza back to the Lord. "Jesus, when our kids were born, it was easy to say these kids are Yours. Help us to raise them right. But, Lord, are these kids really Yours? Help us to give Eliza back to You. She is really Yours and Yours alone. She doesn't belong to us.

"Help me to say as Job did, 'Lord, You give and take away, but blessed be the name of the Lord.' This truth is going to be the only thing that gets us through this. Blessed be Your name. It's the first thing in the Lord's Prayer. Help us to bless Your name first and foremost, regardless of what is happening. My kingdom go, *Your* kingdom come. Our kingdom is so very fragile and crumbling around us, Lord, but Yours is eternal, sure, and unchanging. May Your will be done. As black as this looks, please use it for your glory. Our lives are in Your hands."

When Joel and I were freshmen in college, we had both broken up with people around the same time, opening the door for the Lord to move. At a social gathering that had dwindled to a few stragglers, Joel approached me with a smile, asking tentatively, "Are you going to the Christmas dance at church?"

"I'd like to. How about you?"

"I'd like to as well. Want to go with me?"

As the word *yes* rolled off my tongue, a peace washed over my heart. *What have I been thinking, Lord? He's perfect for me.*

The following day, I told my closest friend that I could see Joel and me seriously dating and getting married. Although we were still young, that was exactly what happened. We dated for two and a half years before we stood before friends and family to say, "I do." In our commitment to serve and honor the Lord in our marriage, we made a vow together before our loved ones to foster a Christian home. We had no idea on that day just how much that vow would be tested. To seek to love, honor, serve, and encourage each other toward Jesus and build our home upon the rock of God's Word. When you're young, how can you possibly know what is to come and the many ways you'd be tried and tested? We were now set on a journey of faith we never could have dreamed or fathomed. However, as it is written, "What no eye has seen, what no ear has heart, and what no human mind has conceived," the things God has prepared for those who love Him, these are the things God has revealed to us by His Spirit (1 Cor. 2:9–10).

The Transfer

Gathering the last of our belongings, I walked with as much confidence as I could to the end of the hall to wait for the EMTs as they quickly began working to place Eliza on the gurney and arrange her machines and wires. The women in the hallway followed me as we came to a stop as a group. Turning to them, I lost the last bit of composure I had. Gasping for air, I muttered through heavy tears, "Shelli, she thinks Eliza...that Eliza might not make it to Children's alive. She may have to be resuscitated on the way...potential respiratory arrest. I will have to get out of the ambulance. I may not be with her. Pray, please, please pray." Huddled together as a mass of weeping women, we prayed with loud tears and cries to the one who could save Eliza from death.

I looked up to see the EMTs pushing the gurney toward us from the far end of the hall and quickly wiped my tears as if wiping away the seriousness of the situation. "If they think I'm unable to handle the ride, they won't let me go with her." Straightening, I put on the strongest face of confidence I could. I wasn't about to let anything keep me from being with Eliza, especially if it meant missing her last moments on this earth.

My friend Diane quickly hugged me. "We'll be behind the ambulance. We'll see you at Children's."

Fastening my seat belt in the captain's chair at the head of Eliza's gurney, I quickly dialed my sister-in-law's phone number in Dallas. "Hello..."

Shouting over the sound of the ambulance siren as we pulled out of the parking lot and fighting tears, I heralded Erika, "Hi, it's me. I'm in an ambulance with Eliza. She's being taken to Children's

Hospital in Oklahoma City. Our doctor doesn't know if she's going to survive. Her kidneys are not functioning."

"Oh no!"

"Please pray! This is so hard!"

"We're on our way. We'll wake up the kids and start driving. We'll be there in about three to four hours!"

Erika hung up her phone and immediately gathered Joel's brother Nate and their sleeping children from their beds, loading them in their van for the long drive north. She called her mother, Sally, to pray for Eliza as Nate drove. Together with a sense of urgency and confidence they had never felt before, they begged the Lord through tears to protect Eliza's life. As Sally later wrote, "I have never gotten on my knees with such great desperation before." After several moments of petition, a wave of peace washed over them both simultaneously. "Did you feel that? The Lord is caring for her. He is with her."

Back in the ambulance, as I hung up with Erika, the EMT looked at me with a gentle smile. "I think your little one is going to be just fine. We had a bit of a battle back there with her doctor. She wanted to have her intubated, but she's so little we didn't want to force that. We figured it would be better to resuscitate her if necessary," she said, feeling around for something.

"Oh no, my stethoscope is up front. Do you mind moving over here while I climb up front to get it? It should just take a minute."

I watched as she crawled over the captain's seat and through the small opening to the front cab. The two EMTs exchanged small talk as she searched for her instrument. *Is this really happening?* I asked myself as I sat staring at the machine in front of me connected to Eliza. If she were to go into respiratory arrest, how would I know? I glanced toward the front cab, silently praying that the EMT would return quickly. The sound on the heart monitor had been switched off, and I had no idea what I was watching for. Looking out the back window, I saw a string of lights in hot pursuit of the roaring ambulance. We seemed to be the only ones aware of the intensity of the moment.

Resentment toward the EMT began to creep into my heart as she crawled back into her position, relegating me to my place in the captain's chair. Was this just another run to her, just another patient?

I tended to believe Dr. White's assessment of the situation over the EMTs. I didn't know anything at that time about "nonfunctioning kidneys," or even what respiratory arrest looked like, but I knew in my heart that Eliza was living on the edge of this world, barely hanging on to the life she had in this earthly tent. Eliza was very sick; I had watched with a mother's heart her slow loss of life over the past week, and I longed for them to see her through my eyes. This was the child for whom I had prayed, who I carried for thirty-nine weeks and longed to meet with great anticipation, along with her twin sister; she wasn't just someone who *might* need resuscitation. *Oh, Lord, she is Yours. Her life is in Your hands. She's not mine. She's not mine. She never was. Thank You for loaning her to me.*

Joel saw the ambulance lights coming up behind him just two blocks away from Children's Hospital. As he pulled over, a strange mix of emotions coursed through him. *I'm pulling over for my own child's ambulance. She must still be alive. They wouldn't be rushing past, with lights flashing and sirens going, if she had died. Thank You, Jesus!*

About this same time in Boulder, Colorado, Joel's parents, Dean and Judy, were driving home from a friend's house, processing the latest news about Eliza, when a roaring ambulance forced them to the side of the road. As they pulled over and shut down the car engine, tears streamed down their faces, as they pictured Eliza's ambulance carrying her to Children's in another time zone, her life in the balance. The heavy rain outside seemed appropriate for the moment, reflecting the outpouring of their hearts as passing cars splashed their windows. The world around them had carried on as theirs had frozen in time, connecting them to events happening in a far-off land. Through tears they prayed for Eliza, that Jesus would hold her and give Joel and me the strength to stand.

The fifteen-minute ambulance ride went quickly as we pulled into the ER at Children's Hospital. Jumping out the back, we rushed Eliza through the double doors, passing a very full waiting room. Joel bounded up behind us, eager to join our group. All eyes turned to watch as the EMT swiped their identification card to open the double doors into the ER triage. From the looks on the hospital staff's faces, we weren't expected. "Where should we take this one?" the male EMT asked.

A dazed-looking nurse waved the gurney toward a curtained area near a storage room. "Our rooms are packed. We don't have any open rooms. We'll just have to put her here. I'll get one of our doctors."

Within minutes, a young doctor entered with his clipboard, looking to the EMT. "Who do we have here?"

"Eliza Schulz, a transfer from All Saints Hospital. Her pediatrician, Dr. White, arranged the transfer."

"What is her condition?"

"Renal failu—"

Before the words could escape his mouth, a tall black man with determined strides and large hands picked Eliza directly off the gurney, saying, "Follow me."

Like stunned sheep, we all silently obeyed. In a strong African accent, he said to the ER doctor, "I'm taking her to the ICU." The EMT grabbed the IV pole and picked up the machine that connected Eliza to her many wires and started walking next to the tall man as he gently carried Eliza engulfed in his large arms, her frame strikingly white in contrast to his rich African color.

This strange man navigated the labyrinth of halls and elevators as if he had designed the aging hospital himself. Once on the sixth floor, we passed through a set of double doors leading to the low-lit ICU. He gently placed Eliza in a patient bed while giving orders to the nurses who ran to his aid. And with that, he disappeared. The EMTs quickly following.

The quiet of the ICU ward was sobering and haunting in contrast to the busy chaos of the ER. As the attending nurse started rewiring Eliza and getting her vitals, I told Joel I should run downstairs to let everyone know where we were. Not wanting to leave Eliza's side, I leaned over her bed to kiss her and whispered I'd return shortly. Joel rubbed my back in assurance that she was in good hands.

After retracing my steps through the labyrinth, I finally found myself in the ER waiting room. I found our friends huddled together, looking confused. "She's been moved to the ICU. It all happened so fast we weren't able to let you know."

Upon our return to Eliza's bedside, a petite Thai woman wearing a white doctor's coat was speaking with the nurse and Joel in a strong Asian accent. She had shoulder-length hair and warm almond eyes that, although tired, seemed to pull me in. "I am Dr. Raven, the on-call nephrologist. I talked to your pediatrician on the phone. Your daughter is going to need to be in the ICU for a few days.

"She most likely has hemolytic uremic syndrome, often referred to as HUS, which is a symptom of *E. coli* poisoning. HUS can cause your kidneys to stop functioning. However, 90 percent of HUS patients recover with full function. She will probably require dialysis while we wait for her own function to return. Her condition is very serious and will require close monitoring. There's not much more we can do tonight, so try to get some rest and I will see you in the morning."

Diane pulled me aside before leaving. "I just talked to Shelli White. She wanted to know if Eliza made it all right. She told me she has never prayed so hard for anyone before in her life. She left All Saints Hospital praying the whole way home that Eliza would make it to the ICU. I guess there was a lot of confusion and politics trying to get her transferred. Children's wouldn't allow her to be admitted directly to the ICU, which was why she had to go through the ER. Shelli was very stressed and frustrated by the whole process. Thankfully, the ICU doctors were helpful to get her up here as soon as possible."

As I glanced at the clock, my body began to feel the weight and fatigue of the late hour. It was midnight, and I longed for rest, but the intensity of the day left me restless. Everyone had left, leaving us to stand vigil at Eliza's bed alone. I turned to Joel. "Well, what do we do now?"

"We rest."

We chose to do more than physically rest. We willingly entered God's rest. Joel and I decided from that moment on we were going to trust the Lord completely. We knew God wasn't in heaven, wringing His hands, saying, "Oh no, look at what happened to Eliza. How did I let that one get by?"

We held to the belief that God is either completely sovereign or not sovereign at all. We also knew Satan had to ask for permission for anything to happen, especially in the life of a believer. He had to ask to do the things to Job, as we read in Job 1:12. Satan also couldn't do anything beyond what the Lord granted permission for.

In Luke 22:31, Jesus said, "Simon, Simon, indeed Satan has asked for you that he may sift you like wheat." Satan had to ask for permission. "But I have prayed for you..." We have an advocate in Jesus! He is always praying for us. "That your faith would not fail." Jesus didn't pray that *Simon* wouldn't fail, but rather that his *faith* would not fail. Jesus knew that Simon would fail Him, not just once, but three times! But He also knew He would work it for his good, as later Peter would become a pillar in the church. "And when you return to me, go and encourage the brethren." Our sifting is never in vain! God allows sifting so we can mutually encourage one another in our faith. It makes us God-sufficient, not self-sufficient, so we can encourage others in their faith.

In Job 1:20, we see Job's response to receiving horrific news, not just once, but four times, one immediately following the other. His world had crashed in on him, and yet Scripture tells us his first response was, "At this, Job got up and tore his robe and shaved his head. Then he fell to the ground in worship." This was pre-Holy Spirit! In the moment of his most dire pain, he *chose to worship* the Lord. What a powerful testament to us! When lightning strikes in our life, is our initial response to fall on our knees in worship of the one true, living God? Or do we allow anger and self-reliance to reign?

I once heard a missionary talking about her time serving in communist countries. A woman once told her that the problem with us Americans is that we have so much heaven on earth that when suffering comes, we assume God is punishing us. In communist countries, their perspective of suffering is very different; it's just a part of daily life. But the beauty for the believer is that God is sovereign and will use it for their good and His glory. What a precious promise!

Joel slipped into a light sleep on a rocking chair near the window as I gently slid Eliza over in her cold metal bed. I lay down next to her, whispering my love to her, trying not to upset the many wires attached to her small frame. I stayed next to her for a few hours, neither of us able to sleep, until Nate and Erika arrived around 2:00 a.m. They came up to see Eliza and Joel before driving me home to our house in Edmond, Oklahoma, twenty-five minutes north, for some much-needed sleep.

My head finally hit my pillow at 4:00 a.m.

When I awoke at 8:00 am, I found my parents tossing on our family room couches. They had arrived around 5:00 a.m., after driving all night from Denver. Since I was up, I offered them our bed. Nate and Erika were still sleeping in Zoë's room with their nine-month-old daughter while their two toddlers slept in the twins' room.

I called Joel, apprehensive of what he might say. Did Eliza survive the night? Was she any better? Joel had just seen Dr. Raven, who informed him a surgical team would be coming this afternoon to meet with us to discuss inserting a peritoneal dialysis catheter.

Restless and feeling locked into events I couldn't change, I walked out the front door, unsure where I was going or what I was doing. I just needed to get out. I reasoned that a good run might do me some good, to run off the stress and adrenaline from the previous night. I started at a slow jog, my mind muddy with emotions as I recalled over and over holding Eliza, unsure if each breath could be her last. Jogging onto a side street just a block away from home, I broke down in a wail of tears. *She could still die, Lord, and I may not be there. She could be dying at this very moment. It hurts. It hurts so bad that I just want to disappear. Have mercy, Lord, have mercy!*

Unable to walk any further, I sat on the curb, holding my head between my knees, watching my tears make patterns on the cement. Cars drove by, going about their daily routine of dropping the kids off at school or going to work. How could they continue on in such a manner when the world had stood still? Didn't they know time had stopped? A tinge of jealously toward them invaded my thoughts. I was just like them a few days ago. Would I ever be like them again? Free to live life the way we knew?

"Shannon? Shannon, is that you?" I heard my name from across the street. Looking up, I saw an acquaintance from church that lived in our neighborhood. Clad in running apparel, she crossed to my side. "Are you all right?" She sat, putting her arm around me. "I heard about last night. I was just praying for you. I certainly didn't expect to see you here."

"I hurt so badly. I just need to cry until there's nothing left to feel."

She sat with me for several minutes, until it was obvious she needed to go. "The kids need to get to school. Do you want me to walk you home?"

"No, I'll be fine, thanks." We hugged as she started jogging toward her home. I knew the time had come to return home, to face whatever lay ahead. Wiping my tears, I mustered up what little energy I could to return. I found myself singing quietly under my broken breath, "More love, more power, more of You in my life. And I will worship You with all my heart. And I will worship You with all my mind, with all my strength. *You* are my Lord. *You* are my Lord."

I showered and drove back to the hospital.

Another day had begun.

ICU

Sent: *Wednesday, September 13, 2006, 12:11 a.m.*
Subject: *Update*

Wow! Again, I'm overwhelmed by the amount of love and support we have received from so many of you. Saying "Thank you" just doesn't seem good enough, but it will have to do for now!

Eliza is still stable, uncomfortable, but stable. She was supposed to have surgery to insert a peritoneal dialysis catheter tube into her lower abdomen both this morning and then again this evening, but it seems to keep getting postponed. Once they have the tube in, they can start dialysis. Until then, she will continue to be very uncomfortable.

But this afternoon, I realized something: if her kidneys would start functioning, causing her to pee on her own, then we wouldn't have any need for surgery or dialysis. Is God allowing her surgery to keep getting postponed in order to allow her to heal without intervention? Please join us in praying that God would heal her on His own power! Pray for pee! My goodness, she's going into her fifth day without peeing! The good news is that according to her blood work around lunchtime, she is slowly improving on her own. God is hearing our prayers!

She has also finally showed interest in fluids again. She ate two popsicles and practically grabbed the cup of ice chips from me. This is really good news! She has not taken any fluids on her own since around Friday. And since she is drinking on her own, they took out her IV fluids! Another answer to prayer!

So for now, the doctor has her scheduled for surgery tomorrow at noon. But that's what they said yesterday, and we are praying that God will continue to intervene in the meantime. Mommy is tired, Daddy is staying with her tonight, and we'll usher in tomorrow with great amounts of faith!

Love,
Shannon

The first two days in ICU were a blur. There was a great deal of activity in Eliza's small walled-off room separated from the nurses' station by a curtain. I remember many visitors coming and going along with teams of doctors and nurses all fussing over Eliza, whose energy level was nonexistent. The combination of no sleep and built-up toxins in her body caused great amounts of pain and lethargy. She was as weak as a newborn baby, unable to lift her own head or move easily. Comforting her was difficult since physical touch caused her pain, although she didn't want us to wander far from her bedside, beseeching us with her large baby-doll eyes.

The best way we knew to comfort Eliza was to crawl in her hospital bed with her, lying still next to her, gently speaking words of encouragement. Oftentimes, we would set her bed in the sitting position, allowing her to rest against us. This way, she could see the activity around her while knowing the comfort of our presence. Looking back on those days, I realize how patient and caring the nursing staff was toward us. We really shouldn't have been allowed to lie with Eliza as we did, but given her condition (we later discovered the doctors held little hope Eliza would survive), they made such allowances for us.

We eagerly awaited the surgery she needed for the dialysis catheter tube, hoping it would offer her some much-needed relief. Since most medications travel through the kidneys, there was nothing they could offer to ease Eliza's pain or listlessness.

During this time, there was much speculation about Eliza's condition and what had caused it. She had the classic symptoms of *E. coli* and HUS, but the cause and source were still uncertain.

During a quiet moment, a young woman with a white lab coat approached Eliza's bedside, hesitant to disrupt me. Her long brown hair was pulled back in a tight bun, emphasizing her studious appearance, which spoke of hours of study. Awkwardly toying with her pen and adjusting her clipboard, she asked, "Mrs. Schulz, my name is Dr. Goodland. Would you mind if I asked you a few questions? I'm a pediatric resident working with Dr. Raven, and although I have copies of her notes, I'd like to keep my own. Do you mind telling me what happened to Eliza?"

I happily spent the next ten minutes recounting the details I could remember from the past week as she scribbled notes. As I came to a close, she shyly asked, "I understand you had been using raw milk and that it may be the source of the *E. coli*? Is that true?"

Taken aback by the forwardness of her question, I hesitantly answered, "Yes."

Adjusting her glasses and moving her clipboard to the ready position, she asked, "Why? I mean, why had you been drinking raw milk? Did you know it carried the risk of *E. coli*?"

"No, not really. I mean I knew it could *maybe* make you sick, but I never realized it could shut down your kidneys. I really didn't know that much about it. I had been using it in hopes of helping Eliza's allergies and eczema. I didn't know…"

"Hmm, I've never heard of it being used in that way. Did a doctor encourage that?"

"No, a friend. I didn't… I mean…there is a lot of very positive things written about it, but I never looked into the potential dangers. But it seemed to be helping my friend's daughter." The absurdity of what I was saying smacked me across the face. *Why didn't I research it further?* The words offered me by my friend flooded back. "If you're comfortable with raw milk, I would try it." *If I'm comfortable. What if I'm not comfortable now? Oh, Shannon, it's a bit too late for that now. Lord, You will have to redeem this!*

"Oh, I see," Dr. Goodland offered with a look of confusion. Forging ahead, she continued, "I also wanted to let you know I called the health department this morning at Dr. Raven's request, to let them know we had a possible *E. coli* case stemming from raw milk. At this point, they don't have any interest in investigating. I was just curious what led you to that decision." Sensing the tension, she offered a smile and turned to go, the beginnings of her pregnancy showing through her lab coat. "Thank you for your time."

"Sure," I offered, hanging my head as a wave of unexpected shame shadowed my heart. *Why do I feel this way? Is this my fault? Did I do this? I should have done more research. But what I did read seemed so positive toward raw milk, even downplaying any possibility of* E.coli *exposure. Oh, Lord, is this my fault? I trust You. I know You must have a purpose for this! But please take these feelings from me before they consume me.*

As I adjusted to look at Eliza, tears tugged at my eyes. *Oh, little one. I love you so much. I'm so sorry if my poor decisions did this to you. I'm so sorry, please forgive me.*

She was just as precious now as she had been the day she was born. *Lord, please don't take her from me. But not my will, but Yours be done! Give me the grace to accept what You have for her. You hold the keys to life and death. Nothing can happen to Eliza unless You will it, and You promise it will be for her good. Let me rest in Your timing.* An image of Jesus walking toward distant rolling hills invaded my thoughts. The sun setting behind Him highlighted His features as He turned toward me, beckoning me to follow Him. His electrifying smile filled His weathered face with joy and love that unequivocally drew me to Him. He turned to continue walking, casting me a glance as He beckoned me on. *I'm coming, Jesus. Help me. Show me where you're going, so I may follow. Please don't get too far ahead of me. Don't leave me, please don't leave us.*

Sent: *Thursday, September 14, 2006, 9:58 a.m.*
Subject: *A new day*

Sleep, sweet relief for all of us! The night before last, Joel was up with Eliza all night as she wrestled around in her metal crib. She tried pulling out all her wires and fussed and moaned from discomfort. We longed for her to have sleep medicine, but since it's excreted through the kidneys, she couldn't have any. She was on her fourth day without sound sleep, and Joel and I were exhausted. Joel was such a trooper, volunteering to stay with her so I could come home to sleep. Then, the surgical team came to get her around ten o'clock this morning. I didn't make it to the hospital soon enough to see her go into surgery, but my dad and I were there to see her come out. A peritoneal dialysis catheter tube was inserted just below her belly button. We were elated that she finally got in for surgery, and when I spoke with a hospital social worker this afternoon, she said it was a miracle she got in so soon! The hospital is currently in transition, moving to a new "tower" on the University of Oklahoma medical campus, so things are crazy. The hospital is currently running with half the OR rooms they need.

Once she was transferred back to ICU, we were surprised to see her attending doctor so soon. My dad asked, "When do you think you'll start dialysis?" He responded with enthusiasm, "How about right now?" Yes! So peritoneal dialysis was started yesterday afternoon just 1.5 hours postoperative. For those of you that don't know, peritoneal dialysis is a machine that pumps a dextrose solution (200 ml) into her peritoneal cavity that sits for forty-eight minutes while drawing bad toxins in her system to itself. The solution is then pumped out into another bag along with an additional 8–13 ml of toxins with each cycle. It's basically acting in place of her kidneys, creating manmade urine.

Since Eliza has gone five days without peeing, her body is very sensitive to touch, and as a side effect, she has insomnia. It should take a few days of dialysis to get most of the existing toxins out and for her to start feeling better. We are currently expecting to be in the hospital for at least another week. If her kidneys have not started functioning on their own by then, we will have to stay an additional week while they train Joel and me on how to administer dialysis from home. But we are praying that God will restore her kidneys to their perfect condition and that we can all go home by next Monday or Tuesday.

They also put in a PICC line yesterday. Poor little Eliza looks like a pincushion from all the blood they have been drawing, and for some reason, she is extremely hard to get blood from. I have had more nurses comment that she is the most difficult blood draw they've experienced. What should be a simple procedure has taken about thirty to forty minutes.

The surgeon tried to put a "main line" in Eliza's neck during the catheter surgery, which would allow the nurses to access her blood without needles. However, the surgeon tried three times and couldn't get any of them to work! So they had a PICC line put in yesterday afternoon in her room. She was put out again while they used an ultrasound to find a good vein. Then a long tube was inserted up the vein in her arm up around her shoulder area and near her heart. It was a rather-bloody and icky procedure. The first one didn't work, so they did a second one, and unfortunately, they have only gotten blood from it once, and that was after five tries. It's the strangest thing; Eliza seems to be somewhat protective of her blood! That's my girl!

Last night, Joel and I took a leap of faith by coming home to sleep. Eliza was so sedated that we felt comfortable leaving her. This morning, when Joel arrived, they told him that she slept through the whole night and is still out! Yeah! She has several days of sleep to make up for. They are also planning to move her out of ICU this afternoon! Praise the Lord! He's so good and worthy of our praise!

Continue to pray for Robin, Eliza's twin sister. She has been wandering around the house with her thumb in her mouth, looking for Eliza. She's still a bit baffled about where her chum has gone. She really only sucks her thumb at night while she's sleeping, so it's strange to see her acting this way. Zoë is doing okay; she's been acting out a bit more than normal, but my parents are loving on her as much as possible. I think they will finally get to see Eliza this afternoon for the first time since she was whisked out of All Saints Hospital Monday night. Zoë has been asking a lot about her, and Joel sat down last night with an anatomy book and explained to her how kidneys function and why Eliza is sick. She seemed to respond well and now really wants to see her.

So for now, we shall settle into our new digs and watch the Lord at work!

Love to each of you. We thank God every time we remember you!

Shannon

Room 3138

Sent: *Thursday, September 14, 2006, 9:59 p.m.*
Subject: *Relief*

Eliza has been moved out of ICU! Yeah! Today was the first quiet day we've had in a week. Eliza has been sleeping soundly since late last night, and that's without any medicine. She has only woken up sporadically as we've tried to encourage her to take some fluids. Our new room is much more comfortable, as we have our own bed and bathroom now. I think we'll be semiliving there for a while.

The doctor increased her dialysis solution from 200 ml to 300 ml in order to get out more toxins. Her cheeks are pinker, and she looks very peaceful! As I mentioned before, we are looking at being in the hospital for at least another week, maybe two, depending on how her body continues to respond to dialysis.

Our current prayer requests are that, one, God would heal any kidney damage that has been done by the toxins in her body, which we were told could lead to high blood pressure problems throughout her life. Two, that she would pee. Three, that she would start to eat or show interest in food. If she doesn't, they will need to put in a feeding tube. Yuck! No, thank you!

We just received information that there has been an E. coli *outbreak from packaged raw spinach. We eat a lot of packaged spinach. At this time, we do not know for sure if Eliza was struck by* E. coli, *but her symptoms are textbook to this form of bacteria. Culture tests have been done on her stool, and so far, they have not grown* E. coli, *which only means she does not have the bacteria in her system anymore. We are still waiting to get the culture test back that show the bacteria present in her toxins. Her body may have gotten rid of the bacteria, but the toxins are what have remained and caused her kidneys to stop functioning. Sorry to all you medical professionals out there. I'm sure I'm not explaining this very well, but this is how I've understood it. We hope to get the results on the toxins tomorrow. In the meantime, I would suggest soaking all your greens in water and vinegar just as a precaution! You know I will be from now on! I think we may contact the health department tomorrow to ask a few questions.*

Love to you all,
Shannon

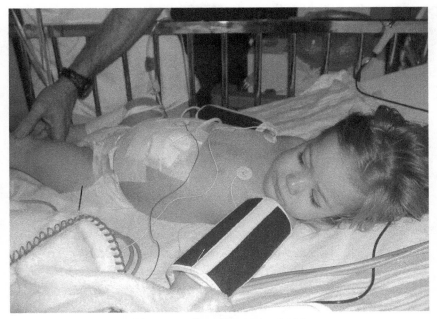

Eliza transferred to room 3138

As I clicked the Send button on my e-mail, voices called from the family room. "Shannon, the news is on! Hurry, they're talking about the spinach outbreak!" Jumping up, I bounded toward the couch, my mind still racing from the many e-mails we had just received from concerned friends informing us of the outbreak.

Watching the images flash on the television screen, I sat in stunned silence.

"A nationwide *E. coli* outbreak has affected a large number of people, and packaged raw spinach appears to be the link. More elderly and young people are showing signs of illness, many are hospitalized, and the number of people being affected is growing. If you have packaged spinach, don't eat it."

Oh, Lord, the green smoothies. Could that really be the source of our madness? Can spinach really do this? I never would have imagined. I remember Eliza requested seconds the last time I made smoothies. She appeared to love it! Could that have really caused all this? Help us know how best to care for her. Give us wisdom.

45

Sent: *Friday, September 15, 2006, 10:01 p.m.*
Subject: *Was it the spinach?*

We shall never know for sure. The toxin test results came back negative today, but both the nurses and doctor were surprised. We began to discuss what else it could be when we realized that they had tested a stool sample that was taken after Eliza had been administered antibiotics. When I took Eliza into the ER at All Saints Monday morning, I had purposely not changed her diaper, wanting the doctors to see it. They tried to take a sample from it, but it wasn't enough for the lab to work with. By the time the lab had asked the ER to send up the whole diaper, housekeeping had come through our room to collect the trash. The next diaper sample they got was six hours later, after she had been on antibiotics.

The health department began to show interest today in Eliza's case since she had eaten spinach, so we began to wonder if we should test one of her diapers from last week. However, the lab specified that the sample had to be forty-eight hours old. We no longer have any of the spinach to be tested. So it shall remain a mystery, only known by the Lord. It does not affect the way in which they will treat Eliza, and that's what matters to me.

Eliza was awake most of the day today, resting fairly peacefully, as peacefully as a two-year-old with wires and tubes from a recent surgery and connected to dialysis can be. She ate a whole (small) bowl of applesauce, and we consider that a success! She also drank quite a bit more water! Yeah! They have increased her calorie and nutrition intake intravenously, so there's not quite so much pressure for her to eat yet. They also did a blood transfusion since her hemoglobin was so low. They were at a twelve count when we arrived at All Saints on Monday, and today they were down to a seven count—not very good. She did look pale to me this morning, but this evening, her cheeks were pinker and she appeared more alert. Maybe tomorrow she'll have some interest in playing or holding a toy of some sort. Her room is covered with balloons, and she is enjoying looking around at all the color. That's really all she can do right now.

She is on her third round of dialysis, which means it's almost been three days! Wow! Each round is twenty-four hours long—where has the time gone? Still no pee! Keep praying that her kidneys will start functioning on their own!

Thank you to all of you who have offered to make us meals! We would love to take you up on it; we now have a friend who is arranging those for us.

On the way to the hospital this morning, I found myself singing along with the radio at the top of my lungs, reminding myself that the Lord is the same yesterday, today, and forever—I have such peace in that. This is nothing new to Him. He's not surprised by our circumstances, and He's more powerful than anything we could ever encounter. May He receive all glory, honor, and praise simply because He is.

Nighty night,
Shannon

*****

Sent: *Saturday, September 16, 2006, 11:59 a.m.*
Subject: *Oh no!*

Robin threw up this morning and has no temperature; in fact, it's really low, which could be a sign of E. coli. According to her blood work from yesterday (yes, they drew blood from Zoë and Robin yesterday—I forgot to mention it last night), she is slightly dehydrated, which is how Eliza began, but otherwise appears really healthy. She has had no interest in water this morning, so my mom is feeding her popsicles to try to keep her fluids up. She had a huge explosive diarrhea this morning, which she has been having since last week. I saved some of it in a jar to be tested. My dad, bless his heart, dug through our maggot-riddled trash can today to find our old spinach bag (expiration date of 9/4). With Eliza in the hospital, it never made it out to the curb—it's the same as the outbreak! My dad is on the phone with the health department right now.

Pray with us that Robin will combat this better than Eliza! We have no confirmation right now that she has E. coli, but my mommy intuition has been telling me for the past two days that she's not right. Now she is beginning to show the signs!

"Because your love is better than life, my lips will glorify you. I will praise you as long as I live! And in your name I will lift my hands. My soul will be satisfied as with the richest of foods; with singing lips my mouth will praise you!" (Ps. 63:3–5). Our hands are lifted high, and our hearts are bowed before our King!

Love,
Shannon

My dad handed me the phone as I sat down in our dining room, steeling myself for the questions ahead. The kind voice on the other side of the line quickly lowered my defenses. "Hi, Shannon, my name is Becky, and I'm an epidemiologist with the Oklahoma State Health Department. I'm so sorry to hear about your daughter, but I'm thankful your dad contacted us so we can help. I have a sheet that I need to fill out as part of our protocol, which means I have to ask many questions. Is that all right with you?"

Drained of all energy, I quietly agreed. Over the course of an hour, I was asked a whole series of questions: "What are your symptoms?" "When did they start?" "What brand spinach did you buy?" "Did you wash the spinach?" "When did you buy it?" "Do you remember where?" "How often do you eat packaged spinach?" etc., etc., etc.

Feeling the exhaustion of the past week, my mind began to wander. I found myself staring out the dining room window, eyeing the peeling paint on our back porch, mulling over our plans to stain it when Becky interrupted my thoughts. "All right, Shannon, I think that concludes my part. Thank you for your help. I'm going to refer your case over to the county health department as I'm fairly confident your family has been infected with *E. coli*. I'd like all of you to be tested for confirmation, as well as the spinach. Someone will contact you soon, but please don't hesitate to call me if you need my assistance."

Hanging up, I remembered the jar of excrement I had saved earlier from Robin. Joel had called our pediatrician to make arrangements to have it tested as soon as possible. Sensing our urgency, she instructed I deliver it to the only outpatient lab open on the weekends at Baptist Hospital, a thirty-minute drive south, ensuring she would do what she could to fax the order to them, in spite of the fact that it was a Saturday and she was visiting family in Texas! Mustering the last bit of energy I possessed, I grabbed my car keys, hoping the contents of the jar held the key to the source of our illness. There was a part of me that needed to know, had to know if the raw milk was the source as the silent shame continued to nag my heart, *I'm off to the lab. I'll be back soon.*

My dad waved me off from a stack of handwritten notes he was feverishly putting together in the family room, turning our coffee table into an executive desk. Earlier that day, we dug through my stack of old receipts, finding the one listing the purchase of the spinach. I also equipped him with the phone number of a friend from church who was a lawyer. My dear father put himself to work making phone calls on our behalf, in an effort to defend those he loves.

Family Night in the ER

Sent: *Saturday, September 16, 2006, 5:14 p.m.*
Subject: *Here we go again!*

We were just told to bring Robin into the ER. She has not peed all day, and she is not at all interested in liquids. We've tried apple juice, popsicles, water, milk, Pedialyte, etc. She has not peed since last night, which is of concern. I've been on the phone with the health department, and it appears that Joel and I may be infected as well. We have been having bad headaches and whatnot but just assumed it was the stress from all this. They have asked us to do a stool sample. So we are on our way to Children's Hospital with Robin. Maybe the girls can be in the same room together.

Love,
Shannon

As I clicked the Send button on my e-mail, a thought shot through my mind like a wayward bullet: *Can I take Robin to Children's?* In the midst of the panic, I hadn't stopped to determine if we could take her there with our health insurance. Since Eliza was transferred there by doctor's order, we knew she would be covered, but taking Robin was a different matter, even though we didn't feel like we had much choice. I frantically flipped through our insurance file to determine if Children's Hospital was a preferred provider with our insurance. Perhaps, given the situation, we could work something out. Frustrated by the mass of papers spread on the floor, none offering me the information I needed, I grabbed the phone, shaking in panic. After waiting on hold for ten minutes, pacing, I finally got the answer I desired. "Are you sure? It's covered? Thank you!" As I put down the phone, a wave of fear coursed through me, the reality of the situation sinking into my heart: it's time to go. *Lord, help me. Not two, please, not two of them! Help me to do this! I'm so scared, Lord! Hide me in the shelter of Your love.*

Running toward my parents, I proclaimed, "It's covered! Let's go!"

As I rounded the corner into the kitchen, I saw my friend Melanie frantically leaving a pizza on our kitchen island. "Your mom told me what's going on. Here, take a slice of pizza with you on the road! You have to eat! Promise me you'll eat, Shannon. You need the strength!" Loading paper plates, she ushered us out the door, quickly running behind us.

My mind was a blur as we drove south toward the hospital, Robin weak in the car seat behind me. Images from the day ran through my mind like a rerun movie viewed too many times. Unrelenting, it began again,; bits of conversation with the health department blurred together with the confused looks the lab techs offered at Baptist Hospital eyeing the large jar carried in a brown lunch sack by a stressed, ragged woman claiming her daughter was really sick at Children's. Their confusion was, "What did you say her name was? Huh, no, we don't have any paperwork for that. What are we supposed to test?" The hour-long wait while they searched for the doctor's orders just to be ushered out with a casual "We'll watch for it."

If our family was truly infected with *E. coli*, O157:H7, the state would need to be informed, which the lab techs acknowledged but didn't seem impressed to pursue. Why should that fall on them? "Call the health department," they encouraged. *We already did! Ugh! Lord, what am I doing?*

I pictured the key to my many questions sitting on a shelf, most likely unlabeled and forgotten. The arrangements to drop it off had been made before I had spoken to the health department that morning. *Perhaps it is better if we wait for them to take things into their hands. Why was I wasting my time?* Knowing my need for answers was driving me, I stepped harder on the gas pedal, as if I could will them to come faster. *Am I to blame for all this? Was I taking things into my own hands with our diet, Lord? I never really prayed about it, just took things as they came to me. Was I trying to keep us from ever getting sick by my own devices? If we just do this or just do that, we won't ever get sick. Is that what I've done? Followed "rules" stemming from a sense of fear, rather than turning to You for all things? Lord, help me to reconcile my involvement in this. Whether it was the raw milk or the spinach, it was still something I fed my children, if it really is* E. Coli. *How is my mommy heart supposed to respond to that?*

> **Sent:** *Sunday, September 17, 2006, 11:36 a.m.*
> **Subject:** *Zoë in the ER too? No!*

> *I must start off by saying last night was probably one of the worst experiences of my life—three children in the hospital within one week?? What is going on? I know I can handle one, but three?*
> *As it is with most ER runs, we drove there in a heightened state of panic just to have to sit in the waiting room, trying to not look agitated or impatient. I waited with Robin for close to two hours before she was called back to be seen by a nurse. Several friends came to sit with us as we waited our turn, mostly to help entertain Robin, as well as preoccupy me with conversation and prayer. Joel had spent the day at Eliza's bedside upstairs, where my parents relived him to come join us in the waiting room. We were all anxious about the outcome of the night. Would Robin join Eliza upstairs, or would we get to take her home? Lord, keep us calm. Oh, why is it taking so long?*
> *Jumping at our turn to enter behind the locked golden doors of the ER patient rooms, Joel and I escorted Robin into her room, which was curtained*

off from another family whose daughter had broken her arm. The next hour was full of explanations to the doctor, labs, and IV fluid since it was obvious Robin was very dehydrated. As we were attending to her, my good friend Nicole called Joel's cell phone. "Hi, Nicole, how are you guys? How's Zoë?" Earlier that afternoon, I realized how overlooked Zoë had become, staring distantly at the TV screen rather than running around, playing like she should be, so I asked her if she wanted to return to the Klassens' home to spend the night. Before I could finish my thought, she ran into her room to pack her overnight bag. She sat on her pillow and bag for thirty minutes by the front door, excitedly awaiting her escort and escape while thumbing through a picture book. I knew she was in good hands, which was why I was surprised to hear Nicole's voice on the other end of the line.

"Shannon, I don't know how to tell you this…" My chest began to tighten as I braced myself for what was about to come. "Zoë doesn't look very good. She won't eat or drink anything, has turned pale, and her stomach is totally distended and hard as a rock. She's been complaining of not feeling good and has a headache. I'm so sorry. I'm not sure what to do. I can bring her to the hospital if it's helpful. I just don't know what's best for her."

I was beginning to feel queasy. "Let me talk to the ER doctor and we'll see what he thinks would be best."

Within minutes, I called Nicole back. "Go ahead and bring her in. They're going to open up the curtained room next to Robin since that patient is just now leaving."

"Don't worry, Shannon. We'll get her the care she needs. We'll be right there! I'll stay with you guys until we know what's going on with Zoë."

Lord, what is going on? I'm so scared! Help us! Our girls need us, but I'm so scared and broken I'm not sure I can do this.

Unable to catch my breath, I turned to Joel. "I'm running upstairs to tell my parents. Joel, I'm so scared! What is the Lord doing? I don't think I can do this!"

Pulling me into a quick hug, he assured me, "Of course you can't do this, Shannon. You aren't meant to do this. That is why you need Jesus. This hasn't caught Him by surprise. He isn't in heaven saying, "Oh, wow, I wasn't on the ball there. How did that happen to the Schulz family? Oh well, too bad they're sick." There's purpose behind this and God's sovereignty. We have to trust that He is going to work this according to His will and glory, and for our good, even though it doesn't make any sense. He doesn't intend for us to get through this alone but for us to rely completely on Him. Otherwise, what good is having Jesus? Do you believe He loves our girls more than we do?"

"Yes," I muffled, shifting my weight in agitation.

"Then you have to trust He is going to do what is best, as any good father would. He's not in heaven, wringing His hands. He knows all things, and even though it hurts like crazy, we have to choose to lay ourselves down, and our girls. Remember, the hardest part of being a living sacrifice is the temptation to wiggle off the altar."

Looking into his face, I could see the stress of the past week etched into the weariness of his countenance. And yet there was a silent confidence about him that seemed to will him to stand with a peaceful assurance that gave life to his words. It caused me to love him deeper and long to hide in the shadow of his strength and faith. Give me that strength too, Lord.

Forcing myself back to the task at hand, I stumbled into the elevator, awash in my own tears. Dismissing the people exiting, I pushed the button for the third floor. As the doors shut, freeing me from the prying eyes of the world outside, I slid to the floor, crying. Why, God? Why? One, I can handle, but all three? Lord, isn't that asking a bit much? Please, You promised to never give me more than I could handle. This feels like a lot more than I ever could have asked for or expected to handle in my life. Didn't You promise me that? "In this world, You will have trouble, Shannon, but be of good cheer, for I have overcome the world." Help me to overcome! Please, I beg you, help me! You kept Job in the hour of his brokenness. Keep me too. I don't want to turn from You, I don't want to live in fear, and I want to know You even in the midst of this.

Picking myself off the floor as the elevator doors opened, I walked to Eliza's room, wiping away my tears. She didn't need to see me this way. It was late, and the halls were eerily quiet, and the lights dim. I peeked into Eliza's room to see my parents watching TV, holding her hand. Seeing my hurt face mixed with fear quickly etched their features. "How's Robin?"

"Um, she's all right. They have her on IV fluid, and we're going to check her bladder for urine through a catheter. Zoë is on her way to the ER." As I explained the situation, renewed pain and fear washed over me as I looked at Eliza lying restlessly

56

in her metal crib, weak and fighting for sleep. Will Robin soon be in the same place physically?

On the elevator ride down, a peace swept over me as I was reminded of 2 Corinthians 4:16–18, "Therefore we do not lose heart. Though outwardly we are wasting away, yet inwardly we are being renewed day by day. For our light and momentary troubles are achieving for us an eternal glory that far outweighs them all. So we fix our eyes not on what is seen, but on what is unseen, since what is seen is temporary, but what is unseen is eternal." Thank You, Lord, *I thought.* You're right, I don't know what You're doing, but I have to trust You have an eternal plan that I can't see right now. Just because Zoë is on her way here doesn't mean You don't have a plan. Forgive me. Help me to cling to the eternal. Help me to focus on what is unseen, not just on what things appear, which may not reflect the big picture. I need You. Give me Your eyes to see. Your ways are not my ways. Your thoughts are not my thoughts. Make me more like You.

As I was heading back to the ER patient rooms, Nicole called to let me know she was just arriving and would drop Zoë off at the door before parking. I had to be strong now, for the girls' sake; it was time to keep my head level and not allow my emotions to rule.

As promised, they put Zoë in the bed next to Robin so Joel and I could run back and forth between them, comforting and attending to their needs. One of the nurses knowing our family's predicament commented while putting on her rubber gloves, "I don't know what all you guys have, but I'm certainly going to shower tonight so I don't get it! You and your husband should probably walk next door to the main ER to get checked yourselves." The fact that we both felt horrible ourselves hadn't really fully entered our thinking yet. We were pushing on, the work before us far greater than any illness we felt. The very thought of leaving our girls to the care of the hospital while we walked next door was completely unthinkable. They'd have to pry me away—that was for certain! But the reminder that we had most likely all been infected and that Joel and I did run the risk of getting worse before better lingered at the edges of my consciousness. What if we did need medical attention? Don't let it happen, Lord. The girls need us now.

The next several hours were filled with both tears and giggles. Robin, having such a silly personality, kept everyone in stitches with her many funny faces and antics. As if sensing the situation was too serious, she made sure to take things in stride. Quick to offer a quirky smile and giggle, even while being prodded by the ER staff. Her labs came back with much anticipation. "Her kidney function looks normal!" announced the attending doctor with a cheer of hope. "We'll continue to give her IV fluids, and as soon as she has a wet diaper, I'll feel more comfortable sending her home. Let's see how her body responds in the next few hours."

Zoë, my eldest and most sensitive to physical harm, did not fare as well. Putting in the IV alone required three people to hold her down as she screamed bloody murder. I'm sure everyone on the other side of the curtain felt for her, assuming she must have been in some horrible car accident, with glass sticking out of large portions of her body, or that she had severely burned skin or some such horrific injury. No, just an IV; that's all it takes to get a good bloodcurdling scream out of Zoë. "NOOOOOO! TAKE

IT OUT, TAKE IT OUT, STOP THIS, AAAHHHHHH! MAKE THEM STOP!" Joel remained so calm and patient with her in the midst of the kicking and flailing arms. I had to walk away and focus my attention on Robin; I couldn't take the screaming and look of betrayal in Zoë's fear-laden eyes. Why did she have to make it so hard? Didn't she know we were just trying to help her? How often have I treated You the same way, Lord? Help me to not kick and scream right now, which is what every fiber of my being wants to do. Help me to remain calm and allow You to work, the Great Physician.

Since Zoë's abdomen was very bloated and firm, a rectal exam was necessary. As one can imagine, the screaming and kicking was taken up a notch, which forced me from the room. Joel remained patiently at her side, holding her and coaching her through, although I'm not sure the hospital staff left unscathed from her kicking. This was followed by an x-ray of her stomach, which revealed excessive gas buildup, causing us to ponder, Why? *The rest of us were fighting typical food poisoning symptoms, nausea, vomiting, watery diarrhea, headaches, abdominal pain, and cramps. Why was Zoë displaying the opposite with major constipation? A second specialist reviewed her case and determined she had a classic case of "backed-up pipes." There was only one option for little Zoë, an enema, which I decided I could not handle staying for.*

Thankfully, this timing coincided with Robin's ever-so-slightly wet diaper, which prompted the doctor to discharge her at 1:30 a.m., with the understanding that if she was still having a hard time urinating in the next twelve hours, to bring her back. Carrying her back to our car in the parking garage, I had to shift her weight several times. It's amaz-

ing how much of our body weight is water. I could hardly believe she was the same child I carried into the ER just seven hours earlier.

Another day complete. When my head hit the pillow at 2:15a.m., I was too exhausted mentally and physically to consider what Joel was still experiencing with Zoë. She didn't get discharged until 3:30 a.m. Joel told me later that she had a really, really hard time, but I didn't want to hear any more. Our friends Nicole and Diane stayed with her and Joel until she was discharged, and Nicole drove her back to her house to rest, hoping her boys could cheer her up.

Joel just called. Robin's stool sample from last night has tested positive for E. coli! *Praise God we finally have an answer! This means Joel and I are most likely fighting the same thing. Pray for our strength and energy. I just woke up Robin, and she had thrown up all over her bed, but she also had a small bit of pee in her diaper, so I consider that a praise! I'm sure the doctors will be monitoring her more often now.*

That's all for now—just keep praying for the twins' kidney function. That Eliza would get hers back, and that Robin would keep hers! Oh, and don't eat uncooked spinach!

Exhausted,
Shannon

After clicking the Send button, I sat back dazed, recollecting the events from the past twenty-four hours. E. coli—who knew it could have such devastating effects? *Thank You, Lord, that we finally have a clear answer, but what do we do now? What does this revelation mean, if anything? The* E. coli *most likely came from something we ate, right?*

Then why do I feel like we've opened a Pandora's box that holds more questions than answers?

Picking up my Bible, I turned to the familiar passages in Matthew chapters 5, 6, and 7, Jesus's teaching on the new covenant with His people. The very first words He spoke in Matthew 5:3 were, "Blessed are the poor in spirit, for theirs is the kingdom of heaven." The Greek word used for *poor* in this passage is *ptochos*, which literally means "beggar: one reduced to beggary, asking alms or destitute of wealth."[1] The application intended is that the kingdom of heaven is meant for beggars of Spirit, those who come to the Lord with nothing of their own to offer, just themselves, empty of self, begging to be filled with His Spirit and life. A beggar only gets what he needs for each day, needing to return again and again to have their base needs met. They are humble and dependent on another.

After Joel and I graduated from college, I worked as the high school intern at our home church. That summer, the students had put together a mission trip to Vancouver, British Columbia, to work with Youth with a Mission (YWAM) in the inner city. The main objective was to see God at work in the most destitute places of the inner city. We served in homeless shelters, gave roses, and prayed for prostitutes on Vancouver's equivalent of skid row and lived life as a homeless person for a day. We were sent out in groups without any money or food for a day in the inner city to experience for ourselves what life was like on the streets. With maps in hand to the local shelters, we were encouraged to eat among the people and to "legally" panhandle to see how people react. I admit it was a very humbling experience. No one was willing to give me money to buy a candy bar from the library's vending machine. Now, granted, my clothes weren't the most run-down, and I might have appeared to have no true need, which was true, other than a day of grumbling for food.

It dawned on me as I was studying this passage that there are true and false beggars in the kingdom of God. There are many who come to Jesus longing to get from Him what suits their best interest. They stand on the roadways and byways of God's eternal highway,

---

[1] Biblestudytools.com, interlinear Greek Bible translation.

begging for this and that, only to reject that which God offers them in response, that which He deems best.

How many of us have given something to a beggar, just to have it rejected? We offer an apple, but they truly long for money, or we extend the gospel but they choose their addiction. If this is true, then the opposite is equally applicable. There are beggars who are truly in need and consider whatever they may receive a blessing to behold; they stand with open hands of need, willing to receive. To be a true beggar before the Lord, we have to be willing to accept whatever He may bring to our open hands. Have we shut them? "Shall we accept good from God, and not trouble?" (Job 2:10). *Lord, I come to You broken and empty. Please fill me with Your Spirit, the living water I need to live and breathe. I am thirsty; fill me with You. I come to You as a beggar, with nothing, in great need of Your strength, power, wisdom, and love. Less of me and all of you today, Lord. Beggars can't be choosers, so help me accept what comes from Your hands as coming in my own best interest.*

Two years prior to Eliza's illness, I had a spiritual awakening of my own. I realized that I had lived my life attending church and doing what was right but didn't really seem to know God. I held my Bible as I attended church and Bible study, without having any real understanding of what all lay inside its magnificent folds. On a quest to know for myself what the Bible held, I began a study of Isaiah. Isaiah 29:13 haunted me, as the Lord spoke about the Israelites. "These people come near to me with their mouth and honor me with their lips, but their hearts are far from me. Their worship of me is made of rules taught by men." Was it possible that I had been merely honoring the Lord with my lips but not my heart? I began crying out to the Lord daily that He would help me to not just give Him lip service but that my heart would be right in the center of who He was.

He continued to work on me. In Isaiah 28:10–13, God admonishes the Israelites again. "For it is: Do and do, do and do, rule on rule, rule on rule; a little here, a little there. Very well then, with foreign lips and strange tongues God will speak to this people to whom he said, 'This is a resting place, let the weary rest'; and 'This is the place of repose'—but they would not listen. So then, the word of the

Lord to them will become: Do and do, do and do, rule on rule, rule on rule; a little here, a little there—so that they will go and fall backward, be injured and snared and captured." Yikes! Was my worship of the Lord like this? Had it only become do and do, a little work here, a little work there, all the while missing the resting place of God? Had I become captured and snared by my own work, offering God lip service while withholding my whole heart? Is it not easier to "do" than to rest, trusting the Lord will work in our lives as we seek to honor Him, which will naturally pour out to others?

God's response was found in Isaiah 30:15, "This is what the Sovereign Lord, the Holy One of Israel, says: 'In repentance and rest is your salvation, in quietness and trust is your strength, but you would have none of it.'" From that day on, I chose to let repentance and rest in God's finishing work be my salvation. Hadn't Jesus said on the cross, "It is finished"? In quietness and trust before the Lord, I have found my strength.

Closing out my quiet time, the Lord led me to Matthew 5:45b, "He causes the sun to rise on the evil and the good, and sends rain on the righteous and the unrighteous." Why? I believe part of the answer lies in Jesus's prayer to His Father, God, in John 17:26, "I have made you known to them, and will continue to make you known in order that the love you have for me may be in them and that I myself may be in them." He longs for us to know Him. Without adversity, would we come? And when adversity comes, will we yield and enter His rest?

We must remember we are all subject to the fall, but with Jesus, all our experiences can be redeemed and used to make us more like Him.

A Lawyer?

Sent: *Monday, September 18, 2006, 10:44 a.m.*
Subject: *Kid1, Kid2, and Kid3*

Kid1: Zoë is doing great, still playing and having fun at her friend's house. We are completely humbled that our dear friend Nicole would be willing to give her another enema yesterday afternoon since she was still having a really hard time pooping. I have not talked to them this morning, but I suspect that Zoë is feeling great today.

Kid2: Robin is doing better too! She has not thrown up yet this morning, and her diaper was really wet! Praise Jesus! Maybe the E. coli is just about out of her system altogether. I guess it can take three weeks for kiddos to get rid of it. Unfortunately, there is no treatment for it—you just have to wait for it to run its course. We are still trying to get her to drink as much as possible, and I'm encouraged that she showed more interest in water this morning. She's going to kick this; I just know it!

Kid3: Eliza is still struggling. She's miserable! They cut down her dialysis to just eighteen hours a day from twenty-four. She looked really puffy and sore yesterday, and we're wondering if they have cut down on the dialysis too soon. Her PICC line in the arm is also infiltrated, which means her left hand looks like a giant marshmallow. They are planning on changing that out today, which means putting her out again. She still has not shown much interest in food or drink, so she will probably get the feeding tube down her nose later this afternoon. Joel and I actually have great peace about this; we just want her to regain some energy, and the IV fluid they have her on now that is full of nutrients could hurt her liver if she gets too much of them. The odd thing is her poop. Poop, poop, poop—that's all we talk about around here! That or pee! I will never again complain about changing a dirty diaper! Her poop has been a really black and tarry substance, much like a newborn's. Sadly, this is unusual, and the doctors are trying to determine what is causing it. They are doing more blood and stool cultures. It's possible she is fighting another bacterium in addition to the E. coli.

Joel and I got to sleep here at home last night while my dad stayed with Eliza. We tossed and turned a great deal but did finally get some sleep. We actually found ourselves crying, praying, and holding each other for about two hours between 1:00 a.m. and 3:00 a.m. The Lord knows all things; it doesn't make sense, but God never promised us it would. He has promised us that He will never leave us or forsake us. I know it must look scary on the outside looking in, much in the same way it did for those watching Daniel lowered into the lion's den, but we can now relate to Daniel—we have such incredible peace, and we trust in our God even more now than we ever did before. He is going to be glorified through this, and that's what we long to see! Justification belongs to the Lord. He will vindicate this situation in His own way and in His timing. Don't be afraid for us or for yourself. He never gives us more than we can handle. We ask that in the same way others were praying for Daniel as he was lowered into the den, you would continue to hold us up in prayer. Pray that we wouldn't allow the potential darkness or lions surrounding us to scare us or cause us to waver. With God's help, we will stand and survive—and thrive on the other side of this!

"I love you, O Lord, my strength. The Lord is my rock, my fortress, and my deliverer; my God is my rock, in whom I take refuge. He is my shield and the horn of my salvation, my stronghold. I call to the Lord, who is worthy of praise, and I am saved from my enemies." What the enemy has meant to crush us, the Lord is using to strengthen us!

Love,
Shannon

Zoë and Robin at home after their ER run. © SRS Portraits

Because of the confirmed presence of *E. coli* in Robin, the health department urged us to all be tested through the Children's Hospital lab, which was outside normal protocol, but given the new sense of urgency, they felt it was best. At their prompting Joel, Zoë, and I gave stool samples to Eliza's nursing staff for testing, which was cleared by the hospital.

The health department wanted to inspect our kitchen, to test any items that might have contained *E. coli*. The most specific was any product I had made with our raw milk (whey and butter) and the spinach, with them requesting the bag itself. We had consumed all the milk from that particular week, so we only had the remaining bottles and products.

Unsure what to do, my dad contacted our friend Mike from church, who was a lawyer. He called Joel immediately to discuss our options. "I really think you should get representation. If it was the spinach, you are going to need someone to advocate on your behalf. You don't want to deal with a large corporation on your own. This would be a case outside my expertise, but I know whom to refer you to. I can set up an appointment for us to meet with him, if that's what you want."

Joel sighed. "I suppose it is. In the meantime, what should we do? Do we give the spinach bag to the health department?"

"If you can, I'd save a few pieces of the actual spinach and freeze it. When the time comes, you may want to have it tested by an independent lab. Also, take pictures of everything—the bag, milk cartons, raw cheese, etc. Document anything they may take."

"I'll see what we can do. Shan's dad dug the spinach bag out of the trash that had been sitting on the curb for a week. There isn't much left, just a few soggy leaves, but I suppose we can freeze a bit of it and still have enough for the health department. I appreciate your help, Mike. I'm not sure what we've landed in, but it's sure a mess!"

Back at the hospital, Eliza continued to struggle. For whatever reason, she was in immense pain. That afternoon, while I was standing at her bedside, she started banging her head against the metal bars of her crib. Disturbed, I pushed the nurse call button. Panicked,

I pointed to her as if her actions spoke for themselves. "Why is she doing that?"

The curly-haired nurse wrinkled her nose. "Oh, the poor dear, she's in pain. I wish there were something we could give her, but the medicines that would help have to travel through her kidneys, which aren't working properly. I know it's hard to see, but this is a rather-common reaction to pain for babies. We can try to distract her."

I placed the baby aquarium on the other side of Eliza's head, pushing buttons, hoping the noise would draw her attention. Nothing. She continued to bang her head. Tearing up, I got down at her level, looking her in the eyes. "Eliza, please stop. This isn't going to help you feel better. It's only going to make your head hurt more. Please, please stop." She looked at me and turned her head the other direction, avoiding eye contact. But at least her head was facing away from the bars, which I considered a success! I was able to keep her distracted for some time as she appeared to settle into a better place.

Eliza hadn't shown any interest in the baby toys the hospital staff had brought her. She was still very weak and couldn't move much on her own. She was also still sensitive to touch and didn't long to be held. As weak as she was, I think we all feared trying to pick her up, not to mention all the wires and tubes interwoven through the metal bars to Eliza. She had a nose tube, heart monitors, an IV, and the peritoneal dialysis tube protruding from just above her belly button on the right side. When the dialysis machine was running, she was tethered. The only contact we could have with her at this time was to hold her hand through the metal bars and to stroke her hair. As uncomfortable as she was, I believe she was content with this for the time being.

Sent: *Tuesday, September 19, 2006, 2:23 p.m.*
Subject: *A new day*

Robin appears to be feeling better today physically, but she's a mess emotionally. I wonder if waking to an empty room is bothering her. Eliza's bed is just across the room from her, and they usually wake up giggling and talking to each other. Once Robin saw me last night as I returned home from the hospital, she started crying, and it took several minutes of comfort to get her to calm down. This morning, when I opened the front door and she heard the garage door open, she started crying, thinking I was leaving.

Zoë has returned home, and I'm happy to see them wrestling and playing together. I'm hoping this will help Robin perk up. My mom and I are going to take the girls to see Eliza this afternoon, and I was told they might all three be able to visit the hospital playroom. Eliza is very weak, but maybe seeing her sisters playing will help. Zoë had to have a third enema yesterday, and we're still waiting for her to go on her own. If she doesn't, they will be putting her on some medication. She appears to be happy to be home, and I love having two of my kids in the same place again.

Eliza struggled last night. She was up most of the night, wriggling around in her bed. She's just so darn uncomfortable! She's the baby that sleeps on her tummy with her head literally straight down. I've never seen anyone sleep the way she does; it looks very uncomfortable to me. So I guess it's good news that she wants to sleep on her tummy, but a bummer that she can't with all the wires and cords that keep her from being able to flip onto her tummy. She tends to whine every hour when the catheter from the dialysis is draining and refilling. She did end up having to have a feeding tube put in her nose—yuck! We just couldn't get her to eat enough of the Ensure protein shakes that are designed specifically for dialysis patients. She's on a specific diet, no phosphorus, salt, or high protein. She has been throwing up some, so we're hoping she will start to keep food down on her own.

Oh, I forgot to mention that Joel's stool sample from yesterday tested positive for E. coli *toxins, which means he's been infected too. No test results for Zoë and me yet.*

Ta-ta for now,
Shannon

An hour before I sent this update, Joel received a call on his cell phone from a man associated with the spinach supplier. After inquiring about the girls' health, he said, "We want to work with your family without having to go into a legal battle for compensation. We are more than fair and really want to help your family. I'm going to send you some forms to complete so we can get the process started. They should arrive in the next week. Please contact me with any questions, and again, please let us help you."

Joel hung up and called Mike. "I think we need counsel."

The following morning, an appointment was arranged for Joel and my father to meet with Mike and another prominent lawyer to discuss representation. As Joel was preparing for the meeting, I typed the following update.

Sent: *Wednesday, September 20, 2006, 8:18 a.m.*
Subject: *My mom's birthday*

Today is my mom's birthday. How I wish our circumstances were different for her! We are getting Indian food delivered to us this evening, thanks to our dear friend and Joel's coworker from India. My mom loves Indian food, so the timing is wonderful. I believe my dad will be running out to buy a cake too. She spent the night at the hospital with Eliza, so I'm madly writing before I leave to relieve her for the day.

Robin and Zoë are still sleeping, and I hope they have a good day today playing and picking on each other. Zoë seems to love pinching Robin's nose to get a response from her. They are both coping with this in different ways. Robin won't let me out of her sight and cries when she can't see me—quite out of character for her. She's angry too. She's been throwing toys and sippy cups. She kicks and screams when my parents try to hold her. I need to be with Eliza today at the hospital since I missed her for the bulk of the day yesterday. So pray for Robin, that she won't feel completely abandoned today. My heart is very torn between the two!

We did take the girls to see Eliza last night, but I tell you, the room was turning greener by the moment from all the jealousy. Robin wouldn't let me put her down, and poor Eliza was watching me carry her around with such hurtful eyes. I could hardly stand it—from either side! I wish I could scoop Eliza up the way I can with Robin, but she's too weak and miserable from the dialysis. It will be a few more days before we can hold her very easily. I did climb up into bed with her to cuddle, and she fell right to sleep—sweet baby. However, Robin got so jealous she decided to lie on top of me as I was cuddling up with Eliza. Like three peas in a pod—I was the one being squished out!

Eliza had an ultrasound done on her kidneys to see what's going on down there. They are still not functioning, but at least they are doing exactly what they would expect from someone with hemolytic uremic syndrome (HUS). I read an article yesterday that said there were sixteen other people affected by the spinach with HUS. It breaks my heart—sixteen other families going through this! Pray for them too!

Eliza's blood pressure is still really high. It was 165 over 100 last night. To put this in light, Robin's was 98 over 50 in the ER, which is normal for their age. But I guess this is another symptom of not having kidney function.

Regarding her nose tube, I have to share this with you. Joel was explaining to Zoë how it worked in the car last night. "Zoë, do you want to hear something funny? Eliza has a straw up her nose! That's how she eats—isn't that funny?" We all had a good chuckle, and Zoë did find it kind of cool.

Eliza has been having a hard time keeping food down. It tugs on my heartstrings to see her throwing up. She also had a fever of 102 last night.

On a sweet note, the Lord has been opening doors for us to minister to other people in the hospital. My dad saw a young girl in a wheelchair outside her room last night, crying. When he asked if she was okay, she said, "Yeah." He pried a bit more and discovered that she wanted to go to the church service that a local church offers in the playroom. When she told her parents on the phone that she wanted to go, they said in a threatening manner, "If you go, we're not coming to see you." It broke her heart, but she wanted to go! So my dad wheeled her down to the service and then "picked" her up again at the end. I believe she was able to connect to many of the leaders, especially one who was also in a wheelchair! Praise Jesus!

I'm off! Here's a word from Joel:

First off, thanks! We certainly feel so close to the Lord in this as we see how Jesus leads us step-by-step.

We are still waiting for confirming evidence (growth of E. coli*) from our spinach bag that the health department is testing. The circumstantial* *evidence seems clear, but a confirmation would make things much easier.*

My work has been awesome. Lots of balloons, cards, a huge gift basket of goodies, an envelope of cash for gas and food, etc. They have cleared my schedule and are doing a great job of caring for my patients. I stopped by yesterday to get some patient notes to sign, take care of some details with the practitioners who are seeing patients for me. It was great to see my friends and "family" at my home away from home, and I think it was good for them to see me too! It's so nice to not have to worry about my responsibilities and care of my patients during this time. Praise God! My coworker Jason and his father mowed our lawn a few days ago. Such a blessing!

Thanks and God bless, you all! Keep looking at Jesus, the author and perfecter of our faith!

That evening, celebrating my mother's birthday around the dinner table with a good friend and delicious Indian food remains a sweet memory for me in the midst of heartache. Joel volunteered to stay with Eliza so the rest of us could enjoy a good meal together. It had been over a week since I had sat down to eat a formal meal, and to my surprise, I fully enjoyed it. My normal propensity for food had been overtaken by the stress and adrenaline of living each moment. This was the first full meal I had eaten in quite some time despite all the encouragement I received.

My mother was rather spent. In our planning, we overlooked how tired she would be after spending an entire night with Eliza, where sleep was virtually impossible. Not only was the spare bed hard as a rock, but next to a leaky window, the nursing staff came in every two hours to start/stop feedings, check the equipment and Eliza, often turning on the lights and unintentionally making a ruckus. Eliza also woke up several times at night, crying from the dialysis cycles. By that time you were so tired you just didn't care anymore; it was time for the 5:00 a.m. weighing and labs before the doctors arrived for their morning rounds. Weighing Eliza required getting her out of bed, organizing her tubes and wires to place her on a scale, and then her labs were always associated with tears. When I relieved my mom that morning, her birthday, she was sent home to care for Robin and Zoë! What an oversight on our part! By the time I came home later that afternoon after Joel relieved me, she was begging for a nap.

Sent: Thursday, September 21, 2006, 9:07 a.m.
Subject: Day 11

Eliza still has a high temperature (102–103), which is worrisome. According to the nephrologist yesterday, if the fever were related to the HUS, it would have presented itself much sooner. We are still waiting on several culture tests to determine its source. In the meantime, Eliza is really sweaty and miserable. She was miserable before the fever, and it now seems to be amplifying what she was already experiencing. However, she did get some sleep last night. Nights with her are generally rough, with only a few hours of broken sleep. If she could start sleeping comfortably through the night, it would make a world of difference for all of us.

The doctors ordered a chest x-ray yesterday, and based on the results, we've ruled out pneumonia—thank You, Jesus! They are testing her dialysis fluid to make sure there isn't an infection coming from the catheter. The dialysis nurse yesterday explained to me that the fluid coming out of her looks crystal clear, which is a very good sign. If she did have an infection, the fluid would be foggy. The only test result we got back yesterday showed a low white blood cell count, which is a strong indicator that we can rule out peritonitis—again, thank You, Jesus!

So the question remains, What is causing the fever? She must be fighting another bacterium in addition to the E. coli. *We are wondering if her PICC line became infected somehow. But we'll just have to wait and see. Once they pinpoint the cause, we hope it will be easily treated with antibiotics.*

Good news, Eliza started playing with toys yesterday for the first time in two weeks! I almost started crying when she reached over and started pushing buttons on the baby aquarium. It's been humbling treating her like an infant when she really is a bouncing two-year-old. Her hand-eye coordination is getting better too. Two days ago, she was so puffed up she could hardly hold her hands up. When I gave her crackers, it took her several tries to get them to her mouth. Much of the extra fluid seems to have dispersed since then. Also, more good news, she hasn't thrown up in twenty-four hours! Joel told me this morning that she drank a lot of water last night, which in our world means five ounces. I was encouraged that her poop seems to be looking more normal as well.

When I spoke with the nephrologist yesterday, she said, "Eliza isn't well, but she's getting better. I am a bit concerned, though, that we haven't seen one drop of urine by now." So keep praying for pee! According to the ultrasound earlier this week, there isn't any urine in her bladder, which means her kidneys aren't making any yet.

As for the health department, our case has been returned to the state HD instead of the county HD. I feel much better about this. We really like the lady we're working with from the state. She has been very compassionate and understanding. So all our stool samples and spinach are currently being cultured. It will probably be Monday before we have a clear answer. I guess CNN reported yesterday that there was an unconfirmed twenty-three-month-old in the spinach outbreak. We don't know for sure if they were referring to Eliza or not.

My dad is returning home to Colorado tomorrow to winterize their house. It's already snowing in the mountains, and he's concerned about their sprinkler system. We've called Joel's dad to see if he can replace him next week—if he can't, those who have offered to help, we may be calling!

"Therefore everyone who hears these words of mine and puts them into practice is like a wise man who built his house on the rock. The rain came down, the streams rose, and the winds blew and beat against that house; yet it did not fall, because its foundation was on the rock. But everyone who hears these words of mine and does not put them into practice is like a foolish man who built his house on the sand. The rain came down, the streams rose, and the winds blew and beat against that house, and it fell with a great crash" (Matt. 7:24–27). The rain fell on both houses!

May the Lord bless you and keep you today. May He make His face shine upon you and give you rest.

Do We Have a Case?

Sent: *Friday, September 22, 2006, 8:33 a.m.*
Subject: *Day 12*

Eliza slept through the night last night! Joel got a good night's sleep for the first time in quite some time! Thank you for praying in that regard. As for her fever, they are treating Eliza for a gram-negative bacterium, which is just a class of potential bacteria that can be treated by certain antibiotics. Perhaps today or tomorrow they will be able to tell from her blood cultures exactly which bacteria she's fighting. The doctor thinks it may be E. coli *still in her system, which seems odd to me since she was treated with an antibiotic in the ER on September 11, when I first took her in. Shouldn't that have killed any* E. coli *she had? Regardless of what it is, her temperature has returned to normal. I guess she was on the verge of getting transferred back to the ICU yesterday. That would have been a real bummer!*

Still no pee, but now that her fever is being treated, we just need to focus on helping her keep food down. Once she shows the ability to do so, they will start training Joel and me on the dialysis machine so we can be sent home. But from what I understand, it's a week of training—so we're still looking at being in the hospital for at least another week. I guess Eliza threw up her milk again last night, but her blood draw went very well, done on the first try with no effort at all!

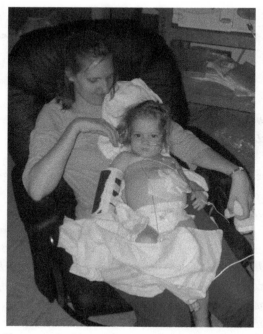

Shannon holding Eliza at Children's Hospital

Robin started getting hives the past two days, and we're not sure why. I called her doctor, and she thinks it may just be an allergic reaction to something, but what? We've been giving her Benadryl. It makes me feel a bit better knowing that maybe it has been the discomfort from the hives that has caused her to be so irritable. She did much better last night after being medicated.

I also had to have a heart-to-heart with Zoë yesterday. She was acting up around naptime. She has been sleeping in Eliza's crib since my parents are staying in her room. We took off the crib rail, and she's using it as a toddler bed. It has warmed my heart recently to hear Zoë and Robin talking and giggling together in the morning. But yesterday I put Robin down before Zoë, and not wanting to disturb her, I tried to get Zoë to sleep in her own room. She started crying and kicking me. I sat down with her and asked her what was going on. She told me that she misses Eliza and just wants to be near Robin. She then asked, "Can't we just go get Eliza and bring her home for the night and then take her back to the hospital tomorrow?" Oh, how it broke my heart! I wish we could! Poor little Zoë misses her sister very much! We talked for quite some time, and it was nice to be able to comfort her in the way she needed.

Please pray for me today as I hear lions roaring. I discovered last night that the other twenty-three-month-old linked to the spinach outbreak in another state died. It seems like everyone else around me knew, and they were trying to protect me. It absolutely broke my heart, and I bawled. That poor mom! Our babies are the same age, receiving the same care. I praise Jesus over and over that Eliza was diagnosed soon enough to save her life. She's going to make it out of this, I know that, but the seriousness of all this has hit me hard. Our babies turn two in just two weeks, October 5. Will they be together here at home, or will Eliza still be hospitalized?

Clinging to the Author and Perfecter of my faith,
Shannon

Later that morning, Joel and I drove into the city to meet with the lawyer Joel and my father met on Wednesday. Why did I feel like I had instantly become the protagonist in a thriller law novel? I had never met a lawyer in the client's seat before, and I felt misplaced.

Joel had been wrestling with the idea of pursuing a lawsuit against the spinach supplier since my dad first called Mike. Was it right for a Christian to sue a company, regardless of the circumstances? We understood the need for counsel in dealing with such a large corporation, but we weren't interested in material gain for ourselves and feared any ensuing temptations and pressures.

I sat quietly with Joel at a large oak conference table, waiting to be introduced to the man termed as the most influential lawyer in the city. Upon his entrance, his tremendous height hastened forward his heavyset body, which he carried with bold assurance. His strong countenance spoke of hours in front of a judge's bench, which made one quickly overlook the graying hair that betrayed his true age. He appeared more fictional than real as he extended his hand in greeting. I thought guys like these only existed in the movies, but perhaps I was wrong regarding who created who.

In a voice much deeper than expected, he announced as he sat hard in the seat across the table, "You need a lawyer, someone who will fight for your best interest in this case, and I believe that lawyer should be me."

As we began interacting, it became obvious this man had earned his reputation. "No one could afford me if I charged an hourly rate, which is why I only take the really big cases, the ones I'm most likely to win. Although, if we don't win, I also don't get paid, which is why I'm going to work hard on your behalf. I could retire—Lord knows I've been at this long enough—but I love the work too much, and I have the luxury of choosing my cases." Calling to his secretary, who also happened to be his aged wife, he requested our file.

We entered into a series of questions and answers regarding our personal information. Upon his asking us our mailing address, I quipped with quick sarcasm, "Why? Are you coming for dinner?" Before the words escaped my lips, I found myself surprised by my own boldness. This wasn't the type of man one trifled with just for fun, but I suppose deep down I also refused to be intimidated by him either. After a moment's silence, he chuckled, put his pen down, and looked me straight in the eye. "Am I invited?"

"No… I'm not cooking these days, anyway. Sorry, my stress comes out as sarcasm."

We spent time going over details in our timeline of events when the actuality of our drinking raw milk came up. "Ah, man! This throws a real kink into this case. Why didn't I know about this earlier?"

"Does it mean we don't have a case?" I asked cautiously, the acid in my stomach turning.

"Not necessarily, but I sure have my work cut out for me. I'm not sure we can defend raw milk use in a court of law, especially if we want to cite the spinach as the source, but I suppose we'll have to wait to see what the culture results hold from the health department. Damn it! This isn't going to be easy."

I fought the tears stinging my eyes. I wanted to run away. I wanted to run from my own decisions, but I couldn't. I was trapped. What was done was done, period. Would I ever be able to pick up the pieces?

Pulling out a pile of articles from our file, he slid a news article across the table. It was about the twenty-three-month-old boy who had just lost his life to the spinach outbreak the day before. Staring at the black-and-white print on the paper, I began to shake. I couldn't control my emotions any longer. I had to escape. Was Eliza's life going to become just another article written in a news journal, like this young boy's, on display for the entire nation? How easily I would have dismissed it just a few weeks ago, but now, it was another mother like me, another boy like Eliza. Tomorrow the headlines could just as easily report the same of us. If this young boy didn't survive getting the same care as Eliza, then what made me think she would pull through? The pain was too much. Getting up from my chair, shaking, I excused myself, fighting the tears that fought for their deliverance.

In an effort to escape, I ran across the street to the public gardens. Unable to breathe, I started hyperventilating as I cried out to the Lord in agony, "I've killed her! It's my fault. Lord, I did this! I did this to my baby! I put her in that hospital bed. I fed her the poison that caused her such horrific pain! How could she ever forgive me?

How could I ever forgive myself? Have mercy on me, O God! Have mercy on her! I'm the one that should be in that bed, not her! Oh, that I could take her place. Lord, smite me, not her! Take me. I'm to blame!" The words replayed over and over in my mind, *I'm to blame, I am to blame…*

I was the one who had fellowshipped with Eve, having eaten from the apple of my own wisdom and understanding. Had I not been tempted by the fruit that promised health and protection from illness and suffering, leading me to eat of its sweet deceit? Hadn't the Lord freed me from that very thinking two years prior?

"When God wants to show you what human nature is like separated from Himself, He shows it to you in yourself. If the Spirit of God has ever given you a vision of what you are apart from the grace of God (and He will only do this when His Spirit is at work in you), then you know that in reality there is no criminal half as bad as you yourself could be without His grace. My 'grave' has been opened by God and "I know that in me (that is, in my flesh) nothing good dwells" (Romans 7:18). God's Spirit continually reveals to His children what human nature is like apart from His grace."[2]

Having grown up in a town where youth and health were worshipped in attitude, both verbal and implied, I carried the pressure of looking and behaving a particular way into adulthood, which came crashing in after the birth of my firstborn. I could no longer maintain the same physical physique I proudly upheld, either by diet or exercise. Because I came from a place where healthy eating and exercise were the norm for happy living and long-term health, my mind had a hard time grasping my new predicament. And yet in spite of it all, my mother stood out as a ray of encouragement. There was a time in my youth when I despised her nonchalant attitude toward her own health. She never seemed to allow the "norm" of society to affect her, appearing content in her own skin, not racing after the things of the world.

---

[2] Oswald Chambers, "The Staggering Question," in *My Utmost for His Highest*, ed. James Reimann (Crewe, United Kingdom: Oswald Chambers Publications Assn., Ltd., 1992). Used with permission by Our Daily Bread Publishing, Grand Rapids, MI 49501.

I went to her weeping over the burden I was carrying in my heart, as she sat quietly processing and nodding her head in understanding. Having visited our church that Sunday, she encouraged me to sign up for the new women's Bible study on Isaiah, which journeyed through both the captivity and freedom of Israel. We had a good cry that afternoon over coffee as we faced the places in our lives where we had both been most affected by the pressures of the world.

The ensuing two months were filled with great trials, as Joel and I literally entered into the book of Isaiah together. After Joel graduated from the prosthetic and orthotic program at the University of Washington in Seattle, we happily moved back home to Colorado for his first year of residency in prosthetics. We had hoped his position would become a full-time job after the year concluded, but sadly, they didn't have enough work to justify another full-time prosthetist. Crushed, we began looking around the state for other opportunities; when nothing came up, it became evident we would have to move again.

Because of the limited positions available for first-year practitioners, Joel determined he should pursue a second year of residency in orthotics in hopes it would increase his future chances to be hired as a practitioner. The University of Oklahoma hospital was looking to fill an orthotic residency position, and we figured Oklahoma was close enough to family in Colorado to jump at the opportunity.

We used the last bit of our savings to fly out for a formal interview, leaving one-year-old Zoë with grandparents. I dropped Joel off at the clinic at 8:00 a.m. for the interview and planned to drive around to find good neighborhoods to consider. Thirty minutes later, Joel called me on a borrowed cell phone to request I come back to get him. *That's strange—it must have been a quick interview.*

From the look of dejection on Joel's face, I could tell things didn't go as planned. He told me that he waited for some time in the front office before the director of the program provided a tour of the facility; after the tour, he apologized for the late interview, saying, "Sorry to have you wait so long, but we were having a budget meeting, and unfortunately, we won't be able to have an orthotic resident this year. I'm really sorry."

Confused and a bit miffed, we decided to spend the rest of our day exploring the Oklahoma City area. In prosthetic school, Joel learned about the Sabolich family and their contribution to the field of prosthetics. Knowing their clinic was in OKC, we decided to stop by to see if we could tour their facility.

We were introduced to a lively young man named Matt, not much older than ourselves, who offered to show us around. As we began talking, it became obvious we had mutual ties to InterVarsity Christian Fellowship (IVCF). Even though we went to college in different states, we had mutual friends from both California and Colorado! Matt was in charge of the residency program at Scott Sabolich Prosthetics and told Joel they didn't have any positions open at that time but he'd keep him in mind. He showed us the stack of résumés he had sitting on his desk of potential candidates. Sabolich had acquired quite a name and reputation for itself in the field, leading many to covet positions in the quickly expanding clinic.

On our way back home to Colorado, we figured our time wasn't a total waste since we met a new friend in Matt. It had been fun and encouraging swapping stories with him. Two weeks later, Joel was offered an orthotics residency position in Florida, which meant another long-distance move in mid-July.

As we were settling into our new rental home, Joel began to show signs of irritation and resentment toward his new position. Within the first two weeks, he knew he had made a major mistake in accepting a position in this particular clinic. He was worked and pushed very hard as "cheap labor" with little respect. He wasn't learning much other than earning money for a company that emphasized patient numbers and end-of-the-month profits at the expense of quality patient care. There were also theological rubs between him and his boss, which often led to accusations and hurtful words aimed at Joel, occasionally painting him in a bad light in front of others.

Any sense of confidence Joel had quickly diminished; he was coming home more and more angry and resentful daily. He wanted out with every fiber of his being, but we were trapped, both physically and financially. He had signed a noncompete clause, which meant he couldn't work at any other clinic within a fifty-mile radius, which would require a move we couldn't afford. The company had also paid for our move, which meant if he terminated early, we'd have to reimburse them $3,000, which we didn't have.

We didn't have any extra money at this time, often living paycheck to paycheck. We had one month where we had to choose between tithe or groceries. That was also the month a check arrived in the mail, a reimbursement check from the state of California for a smog fee we had paid while registering our cars four years earlier. We had moved four times since then and lived in three different states! But in God's way, as we put our trust in Him by giving what little we had, His provision came just in time and was more than enough to supply our need.

Joel was desperate enough that he even considered dropping prosthetics altogether to get a job in any other field that would consider him, but he was also bound to the government due to the stipend we accepted to help pay for his schooling. All students who accepted the stipend agreed to work for four years in the field after graduation; otherwise, they'd have to pay back the stipend funds. We felt pressed from every angle. I began to see a side of Joel I didn't know existed. As his anger grew, so did his depression. One evening at our lowest point, Joel kicked a hole in our bedroom door while crying in frustration. He was like a caged animal desperate for freedom. I got down on my knees, weeping on his behalf, begging the Lord for mercy, as Zoë climbed on my back, giggling. (Couldn't she sense the seriousness of the situation?)

As I was studying Isaiah, the Lord clearly brought us to 50:10, "Let him who walks in the dark, who has no light, trust in the name of the Lord and rely on His God. But now, all you who light fires and provide yourselves with flaming torches go, walk in the light of your fires and of the torches you have set ablaze. This is what you shall receive from my hand: You will lie down in torment." We were determined to do everything we could to trust the Lord to pull us out of such a dark pit. We chose to not complain to our peers or run to our parents for help. The Lord was exhorting us to look to Him alone since we had no light at all, no hope of freeing ourselves.

The day after Joel kicked the door, he received a surprising call from Matt at Scott Sabolich Prosthetics in Oklahoma. He explained that a full-time prosthetic position had just opened. Scott had offered it to another gal who had finished her residency with them, but she desired to return to her home state with her husband, leaving an opening. Matt said he was contacting everyone who had made an impression on him in the past six months! Joel was encouraged to submit a résumé if he still had interest in their clinic. Shocked, and trying to hide his optimism, Joel faxed his information the following day, which prompted Scott Sabolich to e-mail Joel for more information regarding his perspective on prosthetics. He asked him to put in writing answers to several questions about his general care for patients.

That night, Joel thoughtfully labored over each answer, feeling the weight of the influence they could hold over his future. He asked me to read them, which I happily obliged. This was a true moment of testing for me. Joel is, by nature, a rather soft-spoken person who often chooses the quiet corners in social gatherings. He enjoys one-on-one interaction with people and often downplays his own talents, which means he's not good at selling himself. Looking at his answers in this light, I had to bite my lower lip to keep from saying anything irrational. "Do these answers come from your heart?"

"Yes, I believe they are true to who I am and how I see my patients." Fearing his answers might have destroyed his chances with Sabolich, I decided my nagging wasn't going to help any. The Lord would work things out in His way; I needed to trust Him first by submitting to His leading in Joel's life. So I chose to keep my mouth shut by not critiquing his answers.

Over the course of the next month, at the edge of our patience, we heard clips of news from Sabolich. They were originally considering fifty applicants, which was cut in half, then ten, five, and finally right before Thanksgiving, two—Joel and another, more experienced practitioner. The distinctions between them were great; Joel was a fresh face in the field, and the other had been in the field for some time. We figured Joel's chances were slim—who wouldn't want experience over someone still learning?

We had planned to drive from Florida to Dallas, Texas, to spend Christmas with Joel's brother and his family. Joel called Scott, offering to drive up to Oklahoma City so they could meet in person. Arrangements were made for a meeting on December 22. When asked what he wanted for Christmas, Joel empathically stated over and over, "I just want a new job!"

The meeting with Scott went better than expected, going out for lunch with a few other employees. By late afternoon, Scott had offered Joel the position, which was a very encouraging proposition. However, Joel hung his head in defeat as the offer was made. "I can't tell you how honored I am, but I don't think I can take the job."

Baffled, Scott looked at Joel with compassion, sensing the inner struggle. "But why not?"

"I can't afford to take it. If I leave my current position now, we'd have to pay them $3,000 back, which we don't have. I really wish I could accept—everything in me wants this job, more than I can explain—but I don't know what to do."

"Oh, is that all? Well, let me help you with that." Smiling, Scott took out his checkbook and began writing. As he slipped a check across the desk, Joel's jaw fell—he was holding the key to his freedom, a check for $3,000! "How soon can you start?"

Choking back tears, Joel laughed. "As soon as I can get things squared away with my employer and get my family moved!"

That was a Christmas of great elation that will forever remain in our hearts. In a matter of moments, God pulled us from the fiery pit we had been living in, freeing us completely from the financial and spiritual entrapment. For Joel's present, I wrapped a brightly colored sheet of paper with the words, "A New Job Coming Very Soon!" He had received his earnest desire.

Sadly, things didn't end well with his employer in Florida, who took it personally that Joel didn't desire to complete his residency. He told him over the phone to not bother coming back for his two weeks. So we left Zoë and our car in Texas while we flew back to Florida to pack and move in a matter of days. Joel began his new position with great joy at the beginning of the New Year.

As Joel was settling into his job, Scott came to him carrying the answers he had provided regarding his perspective on patient care—the very ones I had questioned. Scott held it up before Joel and said, "I am glad I hired the guy who wrote these answers. I like to say, 'Hire for the person and train for the job.'" Looking back, I thank the Lord to this day for giving me the strength to not nag or persuade Joel in changing his answers. What a detriment it could have been! I learned a powerful lesson about submitting to the Lord and my husband's leadership in our home.

During those long months in Florida, the Lord gently taught me about the dangers of captivity and the freedom He longs for His people. For the first time in my life, I felt free, truly free, from myself and the world—free to love the Lord with all my heart. He had set me free from the need to please others with my appearance or diet. The Lord loves me just the way I am and longs for me to ever live before Him and Him alone. I was an avid people pleaser prior, but the Lord changed my focus from others to Him—I learned to seek His pleasure first, mainly through obedience and trust in His character and Word.

Two months before Eliza got sick, my freedom in Christ had been challenged; like a dog that returns to his vomit (Prov. 26:11), I willingly let my freedom slip by, allowing fear to dictate many of my decisions. Eliza's eczema was very bad, often leading her to scratch until she bled. I was rather desperate to find a solution—instead of sitting before the Lord, I turned to others and the wisdom of man. When I was encouraged to consider raw milk as an option, at first I rejected the idea outright, but as I began to read the information available online, fear began to creep into the recesses of my mind. *How did I not know about this? Look at these ailments they say it will cure. We need to try this. If we don't, we will likely get very sick down the road.*

As one mother later told a panel of women in a forum in defense of raw milk, "By giving your children pasteurized milk, you are killing them sip by sip." So much of what I was reading led to subtle fear—fear that we could get cancer or some other horrid disease if we didn't consider raw milk as an option. The idea that "we need to return to the most natural place possible," only eating raw foods and the like, intrigued the old man in me. Knowing it was a place of weakness, the enemy used it to lead me astray.

Is this type of eating wrong for everyone? No, not at all. But it was wrong for me. At one point, even my dear husband tried to warn me away from it. He knew my propensity toward such things and didn't think we needed to jump to such "drastic" measures to stay healthy. Figuring he didn't know what was in his best interest long term, I continued on. Hadn't I learned a valuable lesson already about listening to his leading? Wasn't I supposed to trust him to lead even when I didn't fully agree? I had gone off and lit my own torch and walked in the light of my own fire.

And now, here I sat in the very depths of my own human folly. *I did it again, Lord. I took the reins, and it has cost me dearly.*

The Lord looks deeply into the heart of us each, saying, "*You follow Me.*" When it comes to secondary issues that aren't spelled out as moral laws in Scripture, we need to be careful to not allow others' convictions to be our own *apart* from the Father, or, more dangerous, make disciples of our own convictions through the creation of secondary laws.

"Our own idealistic principles may actually lull us into ruin. Examine yourself spiritually to see if you have vision, or only principles… 'Where there is no revelation [or prophetic vision] the people cast off restraint…' (Proverbs 29:18). Once we lose sight of God, we begin to be reckless. We cast off certain restraints from activities we know are wrong. We set prayer aside as well and cease having God's vision in the little things of life. We simply begin to act on our own initiative. If we are eating only out of our own hand, and doing things solely on our own initiative without expecting God to come in, we are on a downward path. We have lost the vision."[3]

"A person who has the vision of God is not devoted to a cause or to any particular issue—he is devoted to God Himself. You always

---

[3] Oswald Chambers, "Reaching Beyond Our Grasp," in *My Utmost for His Highest*, ed. James Reimann (Crewe, United Kingdom: Oswald Chambers Publications Assn., Ltd., 1992). Used with permission by Our Daily Bread Publishing, Grand Rapids MI 49501.

know when the vision is of God because of the inspiration that comes with it. Things come to you with greatness and add vitality to your life because everything is energized by God." [4]

[4] Oswald Chambers, "The Patience to Wait for the Vision," in *My Utmost for His Highest*, ed. James Reimann (Crewe, United Kingdom: Oswald Chambers Publications Assn., Ltd., 1992). Used with permission by Our Daily Bread Publishing, Grand Rapids MI 49501.

Broken

Ending the meeting abruptly, Joel came bounding after me. He found me pacing in a frantic, agitated rhythm, weeping. He tried comforting me, but I was beyond the desire for it, wanting to stay in my place of remorse, pushing him off. Unsure what to do, he called our pastor to request his wife call me—immediately! He knew I needed more than he could offer at that moment. They prayed together and hung up.

I don't recall how long we sat in that garden, crying and praying, but I do know that I eventually came back to my senses as I wept for forgiveness and God's grace to endure. The pain of admitting my role in Eliza's illness never fully left me, but I was able to put it aside, as my desire to please the Lord was greater. I wanted nothing more than for Him to be able to look at me and say, "Well done, my good and faithful servant." I might have played a role in getting us sick, but I also knew God was sovereign and wouldn't allow anything to be wasted if I would lay it fully at His feet. *Redeem this, Lord! Redeem me!*

"'I am God, and there is none like me. I make known the end from the beginning, from ancient times, what is still to come. I say: My purpose will stand, and I will do all that I please... What I have said, that will I bring about; what I have planned, that will I do' (Isaiah 46:10–11). 'The storm may rage, but all is well, for our Captain is the governor of storms. He who trod the waves of the Galilean lake is at the helm, and at His command winds and waves are quiet' (Matt. 14:27). Courage friend. The Lord, the ever-merciful, has appointed every moment of sorrow and every pang of suffering. If He ordains the number ten, it can never rise to eleven, nor should you desire that it shrink to nine. The Lord's time is best. The span of your life is measured to a hair's width. Restless soul, God ordains all, so let the Lord have His way."[5]

The Lord gave me an image of a rose garden. As I meandered among the Lord's people, I saw all the beautiful gardens and roses they were planting and tending for Jesus. I wanted to bring such glory and beauty to the Lord, so I looked to their supplies. What fertilizers and tools were they using? Some were more eager than others to give me specific directions. Others encouraged me to speak directly to the Master Gardener, emphasizing His guidance and direction to be their key fertilizer.

Having already made up my mind and rejecting the idea of sitting patiently, I went out and bought my own equipment and began planting. It was glorious—the garden began to take shape, and I saw buds beginning to form on the tender growth. Seeing the Master Gardener enter through the gate, I stood with great pride, excited to share my garden with Him. He was going to be very proud of me and surely offer words of praise, which made me stand more erect in anticipation. The Lord came and stood, smiling at me as He gazed upon the tender growth. *Here it comes.* "Why, Shannon, this is some garden you've planted. I see you've used many good resources, but unfortunately, you didn't seek Me. Do you not remember the instructions I gave you weeks ago? Had I not instructed you to prepare a space in the far meadow where the weeds needed to be pulled and the ground tilled?"

Averting His eyes, I mumbled, "Yes, Lord, I do remember that, but why start there when I can plant seed and grow them quickly here? I have listened to others and followed their instructions."

"Hmm, have you? Have you really listened to others, or have you allowed pride to blind your ability to discern? Have you not read that anything not planted by My heavenly Father will be pulled by its roots? You have followed blind guides, and if you continue on this path, you will both fall into a pit [Matt. 15:13–14]. You have planted flowers that will spring up quickly just to be choked out by the cares of this world [Matt. 13:22]. I'm going to have to uproot these plants. They haven't been sown by Me but rather by your own wisdom garnered from others.

---

5   C. H. Spurgeon, *Beside Still Waters* (Nashville: Thomas Nelson, 1999), 143.

"A garden sown by the Spirit takes time. *You* follow Me and eventually you will have a beautiful rose garden, one that will not be shaken or choked by the weeds of this world. Go and start weeding. That is what I have asked of *you*. Look to me for guidance and I will give you everything you need! [2 Pet. 1:3]. He who is faithful in a very little thing like weeding will also be faithful in much [Luke 16:10]."

Handing me a pair of gardening gloves and His gardening manual, He gently led me to the field where my work was to begin; bending down, He pulled the first weed.

Lord, help me to be about Your business, not my own. Your kingdom come, my kingdom go. Many are the plans in my heart, but You need to direct my paths! Take my hand and guide me, Lord. I long to live in the light of your vision, not others. Forgive me for seeking to follow the leading you've prompted in others' lives, claiming it as if it were my own without consulting You. I know You have a plan just for me. Help me to live in it. I don't want to miss a thing!

In the wee hours the following morning, Joel appeared to be wrestling with our circumstances as he jotted down notes on two small pieces of notepaper:

9-23-06, 3:05 a.m., in Eliza's hospital room:

If this is the spinach supplier (or milk), I'd like to "publicly" forgive and release them from guilt (not fault) and to award $0 for me personally.* I also think it would be funny to say "publicly" that I was going to ask them for a lifetime supply of pineapples for my wife—she loves pineapples!

—Joel Schulz

*To help show that I am doing this for Eliza's long-term healthcare, not for money or vengeance.

*****

9-23-06, 8:36 a.m., in Eliza's hospital room:

The Lord will provide my needs, with or without their money. I don't want a cent. The Lord has also called me as a husband and a father to provide for and protect my family, wife, and kids. So I'm asking them to help me to do this in light of my daughter's medical condition.

—Joel Schulz

On Monday, September 25, Joel received a phone call from Becky at the state health department. She confirmed that Robin's strain of *E. coli* was as suspected 0157:H7, which is a gram-negative bacterium that is commonly found in the lower intestinal tract of warm-blooded animals. This strain of *E. coli* is particularly dangerous because it is part of the Shiga-toxin-producing family of bacteria. *E. coli* 0157:H7 releases Shiga toxins into the bloodstream, which can then damage organs such as the brain or kidneys, even after the bacterium itself has died.

The state HD had requested their own labs for Joel, Zoë, Robin, and my stool in addition to the labs run through Children's Hospital two days prior, which had been requested by the County HD. To their surprise, all our results came back negative, except Robin's, which they planned to test further. It appeared that Children's had lost my lab results and the HD test returned negative. And yet so did Joel's, even though his was positive through the hospital, which meant we never had a clear answer regarding my exposure—although I did have symptoms.

As of that afternoon, the raw milk wasn't growing any bacteria, but there was something growing on the spinach, which would require further testing. There were still many questions to be addressed before conclusions could be drawn. On Thursday, they planned to run a pulsed-field gel electrophoresis (PFGE) on Robin's stool sample to identify the bacteria's "fingerprint" by examining its DNA. Every strain of *E. coli* has its own origin or "fingerprint," much like us, each having our own family DNA or fingerprint. Outbreaks are determined by two or more people carrying the same *E. coli* fingerprint or PFGE pattern.

> **Sent**: *Tuesday, September 26, 2006, 10:24 a.m.*
> **Subject**: *Day 16*
>
> *Good morning! Thank you all for the prayers and support—they continue to mean a great deal to Joel and me. Eliza is still struggling. We often seem to have two steps forward and one step backward. Yesterday was one of those days, but I'm hoping today will look brighter. Eliza looked great over the weekend, and I began to envision her coming home soon, but it's still too early in the week to tell. Saturday evening, she was all a-twitter with smiles, and very playful. Our pastor, his wife, and a few elders came to anoint Eliza with oil and pray over her. Afterward, she was throwing a foam football to one of them—actually, she was just throwing it up in the air, and it usually came back to hit her on the head! But she thought it was great fun. After about an hour of playing, she crashed hard from exhaustion, but to see her behaving more like herself was a small piece of heaven for me.*
>
> *Late Saturday night, while Joel was sleeping, she pulled out her feeding tube. Since she had been eating well on her own, the doctor decided on Sunday not to put it back in—another wonderful advancement. However, since then she has slowly declined. Yesterday was very frightening for me as she was so weak and shaky she couldn't feed herself a cracker. I had to hold her head up for her since her body is still as limp as a newborn baby's, and she was unable to get her hand to reach her mouth. It was very disturbing to see. How did she go from Saturday*

night to this? She's also madder than a hornet! With the limited energy she does have, she spends her time thrashing around in her big metal crib, banging her head against the railings while kicking her feet in the air. Again, very disturbing! Where has this come from? Sadly, she wouldn't let me comfort her. She was either sleeping or thrashing around. I finally had to leave since I couldn't emotionally handle it.

The law office, as if on cue, chose this day to take video footage of me caring for Eliza in her hospital room. I believe they got more than they bargained for since Eliza batted at me with both arms when I tried to pick her up, and when I finally did subdue her, she was so wiggly I had to put her back down. Not one of our finer moments—all captured on video. I had made the decision from early on to not allow cameras in Eliza's room. I didn't want to remember those early days. We were just trying to survive, and if we did lose her, I didn't want it memorialized for our reliving later.

Joel and I had to make a few hard choices yesterday regarding Eliza's health. We decided to have the feeding tube put back in. We're hoping the protein shake will help her regain energy. She's been eating solids, but not drinking anything, and we wonder if that's why she's so weak. We also decided to have another PICC line put in—her third one. The IV she has now (her fifth one) is wearing out, and if her kidneys start to function (oh, I hope and pray so) this week on their own, we can bring her home with a PICC line, but not with the IV. She has been on antibiotics for five days now to get rid of the fever she had but still has five days of treatment remaining. It turned out she had a common hospital infection called pseudomonas, easily treated by antibiotics. Her fever is completely gone, and we could bring her home with the PICC line to keep administering the antibiotics, which are administered intravenously, so we're trying to think ahead.

Our new focus will be trying to get her to drink more fluid. She's eating well but refuses to drink anything. Of course, she won't be sent home until she's doing both well. We are supposed to start training on the dialysis this week, but so far, no one has mentioned anything to us personally. So we are looking at next Monday at the earliest to get her home, unless those kidneys start functioning on their own. So far, her blood work has not budged in that regard.

Joel's dad arrived late Sunday night and is basically living at the hospital for us. Joel returned to work yesterday, and I'm going back and forth between home and hospital. My sister Heather will be arriving later this week from Denver to replace my mom, who will return to help my father in Colorado.

We took the girls to see Eliza yesterday for the first time in over a week. We were able to take Eliza down to the playroom—it was the first time she's left her room! We were able to stop her dialysis cycle for an hour so she could venture out. She was so weak; I just laid her on the floor while Robin tried to play with her. Robin and Zoë appeared to enjoy themselves.

You know you're an emotional mess when you cry at a movie like Cars! *It's just a silly race car!*

Love,
Shannon

*****

Sent: *Thursday, September 28, 2006, 9:17 a.m.*
Subject: *Brokenness*

I wish Joel would write this e-mail for me as I've reached the point of pure brokenness. He would probably write it in a much more matter-of-fact manner, but you're stuck with me, a broken mom.

Yesterday was a very hard day. We started our dialysis training. Joel couldn't be there due to work, so it was just my mom and me. I sat down with the dialysis nurse as she began to explain the first steps of training. I began asking her questions, such as, "What should we do with all the dialysis equipment once Eliza's kidneys begin functioning again?" "Will the catheter need to be removed surgically?" etc. She looked me square in the eyes and said very firmly, "You do realize that by this point, if she hasn't gotten her kidney function back, she's probably not going to. You are looking at doing this for a very long time, so I need you to pay attention to what I'm trying to teach you." My heart sank through the floor, and I became nauseas. I pulled myself together as much as possible, but honestly, I only caught small blurbs of what she was saying. I caught things like, "No more baths or swimming pools," "Most parents put a small egg timer in the kitchen to time themselves when washing their hands," "You can't touch anything but the dialysis tube once they're clean," "You'll need to scrub down the area near the dialysis machine once a day..." How did my life come to this?

Once she finally left the room, my mom and I broke down in tears. We concluded that she's just a nurse; we really needed to talk to the doctor personally before jumping to conclusions. I had the doctor paged, and he arrived shortly thereafter. I asked him outright, "We've been told from the beginning that

Eliza had a 90 percent chance of regaining kidney function and that it was just a matter of time. Why did the nurse say what she did?" He told me in the most compassionate way he could that the nurse was right. "Eliza has gone almost three weeks on dialysis without any change in her creatinine levels [what is excreted from the kidneys]." Normal kidney function has a 0.4–0.7 creatinine level, and Eliza has been at 5 (no kidney function) since she arrived at the hospital. He said that by now they should have seen some change in that number. Each day that goes by without any change in that number, she continues to slip out of the 90 percent who recover full kidney function. He said that he hadn't given up on her entirely, though. "I'm going to give her until four weeks [two weeks from now] on dialysis before I'm ready to say that she's not going to regain any function. At that point, we'll do some more tests to determine what we're looking at. Then we'll discuss her future options, such as long-term dialysis and/or possibly a kidney transplant." I almost passed out at this point.

How did I get here?

Since I had been riding on the fact that 90 percent of HUS patients recover fully, I had completely closed the door in my mind on these "other options." I had not only closed the door but had also taped over it with caution tape: DO NOT ENTER! *Yesterday, the nurse barged through that door, and the doctor gently began to peel off the tape. However, there's a part of me that still does not want to accept it! I've even begun to shut the door again in my mind, and yet now I fear it being forced open again. I hit a wall last Friday that I was still trying to stand up from. I was probably on my knees when this news knocked me out flat on my back. I'm lying in front of that door, trying to keep it shut—if I just lie here, they won't be able to open it, right? God, please make this go away! I want my baby back whole and complete! I want her to be a normal kid able to do normal kid things.*

The other concern the doctor mentioned yesterday is the fact that the toxins that attacked Eliza's kidneys also attacked her whole body, including her brain. Most people recover fully, but again there are some concerns with Eliza. She has muscle twitching that the physical therapist said isn't a normal part of muscle atrophy. She's also not acting quite like herself—in the same way she was last week. The doctor said he's not ready to do an MRI yet but wants us to monitor her closely to inform him of any changes in her responsiveness. I'm not sure what all this means yet.

To add insult to injury, our car stopped working yesterday. But in God fashion, I made it home. It died in the driveway as I was waiting for the garage door to open. A friend of ours who is traveling this weekend lent us their second car—now that's a friend! Thank you!

We are experiencing a change in personnel today. My mom flew home this morning to be with my dad—she needed a well-deserved break! Man, that woman has cleaned our house, done our laundry, ironed our clothes, and taken care of two crazy kids. She has been a lifesaver! But we also realize that we aren't ready to do this on our own, so my sister Heather is flying in this afternoon with her three-month-old son, Aiden. She and Joel's dad will be helping until next Tuesday, when my parents will return to stay until the end of October. Joel's dad has been living at the hospital for us, and I'm forever grateful for his presence and the freedom to walk away when it gets to be too much.

Joel is doing great—he's a rock! His strength through all this has kept me going. As he put it, "I don't expect Eliza to regain kidney function, but I'm sure putting my hope in that it will." I guess that's the difference between us. I put my expectations in that she would be better by now, whereas Joel has had no expectations, just great hope. In the past ten years, he has become one amazing man, and I'm very thankful to be at his side.

I've been singing along to one of my favorite songs by a musician we met in college, Danny Oertli. "Where can I go to meet with You, Lord? My soul is so thirsty for You. Send forth Your truth as I worship You with tears. I am broken. I have nothing to give as I fall at your feet and worship You with tears."

Broken and nauseas before you,
Shannon

In John 6:52–71 we see an interesting account of Jesus teaching the disciples a really hard concept to accept. He was telling them, "I tell you the truth, unless you eat the flesh of the Son of Man and drink his blood, you have no life in you. Whoever eats my flesh and drinks my blood has eternal life, and I will raise him up at the last day. For my flesh is real food and my blood is real drink. Whoever eats my flesh and drinks my blood remains in me, and I in him."

On hearing it, many of his disciples said, "This is a hard teaching. Who can accept it?" The Scripture tells us that "many of his disciples turned back and no longer followed him." Jesus turned to His most intimate twelve and asked, "You do not want to leave, too, do you?"

I love Peter's heart in this moment. Knowing he didn't understand Jesus's teaching, he looked beyond his own understanding to the man he knew and His character. He turned and said, "Lord, to whom shall we go? You have the words of eternal life. We believe and know you are the Holy One of God."

Of course, we can look back at these passages with foreknowledge, knowing Jesus is speaking about communion and the need to be identified in His flesh and blood on the cross, which was poured out for our salvation. But at that time, this sounded like the words of a madman. Why would God want men to become cannibals? It didn't make sense.

There are going to be times in our life when Jesus will turn to us with the same question, "I know you don't understand this teaching, I know it seems crazy right now, but you won't leave me too, will you?" We need to trust that hard teachings may not make sense today, but God will reveal the meaning in time. The question remains, Will you walk away because you don't understand, or will you remain in Me so that I can reveal these things to you in *My* time?

It was during this dark time that I felt this piercing question from the Lord, "Shannon, I know this doesn't make sense, and I know it goes against what you think is right. Nevertheless, you won't leave Me too, will you?"

I chose to join in fellowship with Peter. "Lord, to whom shall I go? You have the words of eternal life, and I believe and know you are the Holy One of God. I will choose to trust you!"

"If a person is ever going to do anything worthwhile, there will be times when he must risk everything by his leap in the dark… Trust completely in God, and when He brings you to a new opportunity of adventure, offering it to you, see that you take it. We act like pagans in a crisis—only one out of an entire crowd is daring enough to invest his *faith* in the character of God."[6]

After picking Heather up from the airport, we drove to the hospital to spend a few minutes with Eliza before driving home. I needed to drop Heather off, give her a quick rundown before returning back to the hospital so Joel and his father could have dinner together.

---

[6] Oswald Chambers, "Yes—But…!" in *My Utmost for His Highest*, ed. James Reimann (Crewe, United Kingdom: Oswald Chambers Publications Assn., Ltd., 1992). Used with permission by Our Daily Bread Publishing, Grand Rapids MI 49501. All rights reserved.

They really hadn't had much time to connect, and I felt they both deserved a night off from hospital duty.

Joel had received a follow-up call from Becky at the state HD that afternoon, which I was sure they'd want to discuss. She was quite surprised and flustered by the PFGE results from Robin's *E. coli*. The DNA didn't match the strain from the nationwide spinach outbreak. Two enzymes didn't match, and five isolates were off in one band, and four in another in comparison, which means we couldn't be considered part of the major outbreak.

The spinach had also not grown any *E. coli*, and the milk products had been cleared, but their results were questioning, causing wonderment by the HD epidemiologists. These were not the results they were expecting. However, they were comparing their results to other *E. coli* patterns from previous cases.

We also couldn't be considered an Oklahoman outbreak since the HD only had one positive *E. coli* test from Robin. If they could have accessed the lab results for Joel from the hospital, we could have been considered worthy of attention, but sadly, his labs had been swept under the rug due to hospital protocol. As far as they were concerned, our case was closed. There wasn't anything left for them to pursue. Feeling lost to the world of bureaucracy and lack of communication between the county and state HD, we turned our focus back to Eliza.

Hope

I was just beginning to settle myself into the evening when one of the nurses encouraged me to enjoy a free hamburger from the cafeteria. She sat with Eliza until I returned. My mind was still ruminating over the test results from the health department as I ate. Would we ever know for certain the origin of our illness? The circumstantial evidence didn't make sense in light of the testing.

I hate milk, always have—just ask my mother, who spent hours trying to get me to drink milk as a child, all to no avail. I had recently been sick but didn't drink milk, and Zoë didn't appear sick, but she does drink milk. We all had the spinach smoothie; Eliza had seconds, but I remember Zoë only had a small sip and didn't like it. I wasn't particularly fond of it either, so I didn't make her finish it, but I drank most of mine. Joel and Robin had theirs. The lot number on our spinach bag was one off from the main outbreak with the same expiration date, so therefore, the spinach made the most sense, right?

Although the HD tests from the milk had been questionable. Why? My friend's daughter had been sick when I picked up the milk from her, and she was adamant about not telling my doctor. Had she been hiding something from me? Images of the dirty barn refrigerator where we picked up the milk came to mind. It was an old model aged with barn wear. Could we have picked something up from the milk bottle themselves? Perhaps they had become infected during packaging or processing? But the plaguing question that nagged me was, Why hadn't others come forward in either case, whether it was the spinach or milk? Why did we stand alone?

One week prior, news had broken of an *E. coli* outbreak in California associated with raw milk from a large chain supplier. Six people had gotten sick, and two children were hospitalized with

HUS. Reading the article made my stomach turn. Was this proof that it *was* possible to get *E. coli* from raw milk? Why couldn't I wrap my mind around it? Why was it so hard to believe? Contradictions from many of the resources that touted its health benefits and safety that I had read months before played in my mind. The words from a friend when Eliza had first become sick also replayed over and over, "Don't trust the health department. They only want to shut the farm down." *Why would they want to do that unless there was reason?* They had been nothing but helpful and supportive toward our family.

A few days prior, I had received a puzzling phone call from a man associated with a large raw milk advocacy group. He also had direct connection to the milk supplier in the California *E. coli* outbreak. He had called on behalf of the farmer from whom we had bought our milk. "He is worried sick and wants to know if you have any intention of suing him." *Suing him? What on earth would I do with a farm? The very thought of Joel and I owning a farm is laughable. We who are allergic to all things farm—horses, cows, hay, perhaps even the tractors!* "No, we have no intention of suing. We have no interest in his farm or causing his family grief."

"Ah, that's a relief to hear. I'm sure he'll be glad to hear that."

Still wrestling with many questions, I asked him sheepishly, "Since you know what's going on in California, is it possible to get *E. coli* from raw milk?"

I was immediately taken aback by his sudden change in demeanor as he said, seething, "They have no way of proving that."

"That's not what I'm asking. I need to know if it's possible to get sick from raw milk."

"They can't prove that!" he boomed back again. As if realizing what he had done, he quickly ushered himself off the phone with great agitation. "Again, I'm really sorry about your daughter." *Click.* *What was that?*

I just wanted to know if he thought it was possible for a person to get sick from raw milk, but instead I got an angry reply about how it couldn't be proven. My confidence in the safety of raw milk certainly didn't grow; if anything, it made me question further. Was he unintentionally saying someone could get sick from the milk but it could never be proven, which allows them to continue touting its safety? And if so, where does that leave me? Or those two kids in California fighting for their lives?

I was beginning to feel like a pawn caught between the raw milk advocates and the health department—one trying to protect their rights by exaggerated safety, discounting anyone who could be sick, and the other becoming overcautious to protect as many people as possible since the safety record wasn't complete. The cat-and-mouse game was being played out right in front of me.

Upon my return to Eliza's room, I was surprised to see a group of ladies from our church mingling in the hall. What a treat to fellowship with others! Visitors meant a great deal to us. I know they often didn't know what to say, but we weren't looking for words; we were looking for love—a hug, a warm smile, extending a hot cup of coffee, and encouragement that Jesus loves us. We just needed to know we hadn't been forgotten; to see the outside world willing to enter into our brokenness always lifted our spirits.

I noticed that Joel's dad had left two dirty diapers folded up on the supply table in Eliza's room. We gave each of her diapers to the nurses daily for weighing. It was one way we measured if she was urinating or not. For weeks, her diapers had remained dry and weightless, which made me wonder why these two had been separated.

When Joel and his father returned from dinner, I saw them speaking to one of the nurses while I continued fellowshipping with our visitors. Eliza's diaper was also changed, furthering my interest. I sensed something was happening. A few moments later, the nurse returned, beaming from ear to ear. Joel's father looked at her with a tear in his eye, and Joel's countenance changed. "What, what is going on?" I couldn't take it anymore—what did they know?

Looking at me, they both exclaimed, "She had a wet diaper!"

"What?" I almost fell over. "What are you saying? She's peeing again?" The excitement was making it hard to think straight as I stood in bewildered confusion.

"Well," Joel's dad offered, "a little bit. I've had my suspicions since last night, but I couldn't get it confirmed until now. It's not much, but it's certainly something!" His eyes could no longer hide his skepticism—he was positively beaming! Joel came to me, and we hugged in stunned silence, which quickly melted into tears. When I let him go, he started moaning like a baby in his deeply felt sobbing—he almost couldn't stand from the weight of it. Seeing him made me weak and cry even harder. Our friends joined in the celebration, everyone hugging and crying. Wasn't this the moment we'd been waiting for? But what did it mean? Was Eliza better?

"No person, devil or conceivable thing is able to snatch us from His hand. Under no circumstances can anyone, by any scheme, remove us from being His favorites, His property, and His protected children. What a blessed promise!"[7]

> **Sent**: *Thursday, September 28, 2006, 10:20 p.m.*
> **Subject**: *She peed!*
>
> *Finally, some good news—she peed! We have no idea what this means, as it happened this evening after the doctors had left for the day, but I only know of one way for a person to make pee, and that's through the kidneys! She peed! Thank God Almighty, she peed! Joel bawled like a baby. I stood around shocked. I'll have to share more later, after we talk to the doctor tomorrow, but for now, I think Joel and I will get the first night of sound sleep we've had in three weeks. Also, Eliza was examined today by a neurologist to check her muscle twitching. She didn't think there was anything to worry about. So we take it her brain is functioning just fine. Much love and appreciation for each and every one of you!*
>
> *Worn out and finally at peace,*
> *Shannon and Joel*

---

[7]   C. H. Spurgeon, *Beside Still Waters* (Nashville: Thomas Nelson, 19991), page 227.

Sent: *Friday, September 29, 2006, 8:47 a.m.*
Subject: *Joel's yesterday*

Hello and love to you all!

Joel here.

   Yesterday was very hard for me! I found out that it would take a week to get the dialysis machine and supplies shipped to our house, so Eliza would need to stay at least one more week in the hospital, definitely missing her and Robin's birthday on the fifth. My father had mentioned two potential, possibly, slightly damp diapers from the night before. One diaper weighed ten grams more than a dry diaper, and the other one was eleven grams more. A milliliter of water weighs 1 gram, so a soda can weighs about 350 grams. Eliza's "wet" diapers contained less than one-thirty-fifth of a can of soda—less than half a thimbleful!

   Last night's diaper had about forty grams, equaling about two ounces or one quarter cup!

   I was exhausted all yesterday, and my dad and I decided to not tell Shannon about the potential "pee" to not create false hopes for her until we knew for sure. I was waiting all day long for a doctor confirmation, but we never got one. Also, our Honda car stopped when I tried to pull out of Children's parking lot when my dad and I were going to dinner! Thank God we had two cars there, and a mechanic friend can stop by today to get our car moving again.

   Well, anyway, now it was my turn to be broken.

   I can relate to a piece of metal that is being polished. Sometimes, even after all the cutting, shaping, filing, and sanding, when the metal is being polished, the craftsman sees a scratch. Now he goes back to the grindstone to remove a thin layer of material to get it smooth again. How that metal must want to resist having the smooth polishing cloth with the warmth of the hands of the craftsman taken away, only to be pushed up against the hard, loud, sparking-hot surface of the grindstone. That was my yesterday. However, last night's news of pee brought me back to the smooth polishing cloth, and I cried like a baby when I heard.

After Shannon left, and crying some more mixed tears of sorrow, exhaustion, relief, and joy with my papa, I decided I needed to run a "victory lap" for Eliza by relieving my own bladder. When I came out of the bathroom, my dad was holding her, and I thought she was asleep. I said good night to my papa, and as I was leaving, Eliza said, "Dat-dee," daddy, with a smile on her face and looking right at me. Tears of joy streamed down, and I ran back to her and held her little hand. Again, "Dat-dee, Dat-dee!" with smiles on all faces. I said, "Eliza, give me five!" And even with her soft arm immobilizer on (to prevent her from bending her elbow near the IV site), she managed to slap me five! That made my night!

Obviously, we still need to see what this means after talking with the doctor, but it is great news!

The Lord may not be through with me yet, but I pray that when He is finished, at the end of my life, He can see His own face reflected in the mirror He gives me through the polishing process for His own glory!

Not that I have already obtained all this, or have already been made perfect, but I press on to take ahold of that for which Christ Jesus took ahold of me. Brothers, I do not consider myself yet to have taken ahold of it. But one thing I do: forget-ting what is behind and straining toward what is ahead, I press on toward the goal to win the prize for which God has called me heavenward in Christ Jesus (Phil. 3:12–14).

Because of the Lord's great love, we are not consumed, for His compassions never fail. They are new every morning (and sometimes even at night!). Great is Your faithfulness. I say to myself, "The Lord is my portion; therefore I will wait for him" (Lam. 3:22–24).

Press on to Jesus!

Joel

Joel with Eliza at Children's Hospital. © Traina Photography

Sent: Saturday, September 30, 2006, 10:00 a.m.
Subject: Not out of the woods—yet

Thank you so much for rejoicing with us as we've seen God moving, but I'm sad to say that we're not out of the woods yet. Eliza's creatinine output is still not great even though she peed (in fact, I think it got worse)—meaning, it will be a while before we know the true condition of her kidneys. There are children who pee small amounts but still require long-term dialysis. So keep praying with us! We certainly took a step in the right direction, but we're still on pins and needles. Eliza did pee again yesterday morning, but it was a very small amount—forty grams Thursday night, and twenty-seven yesterday morning.

In the meantime, Joel and I are still proceeding with the dialysis training, and the equipment is still scheduled to ship to our house. Pray for more and more pee and that her kidney function will continue to strengthen with each passing day. It was explained to us a while back that when the toxins attacked Eliza's kidneys, it caused all the blood to swell around the outer walls of her kidneys. It's much like forming a scab when you scrape yourself. It takes time for the scab to peel and fall away—that's what we've been waiting for all this time—for that scab to fall away so her kidneys could function normally again. So perhaps we're starting to see the beginning signs of small bits falling away, or it could be that large parts of her kidneys are dead, overwhelmed by the swelling and damage.

We are still looking at being in the hospital for another week or more, unless Eliza miraculously starts peeing lots more in the next few days. So our joy is guarded and cautious at this point. She still has no interest in liquid at all! She won't drink a thing. They cut back her tube feeding to just at night, which is good, but now she's not getting as much fluid. Pray that her interest would increase—we need her to start drinking! How can she pee if she won't drink? The physical therapist told me that the throat muscles are the hardest to get back. It's probably painful for her to swallow right now—liquids are the hardest substance for throat muscles to control, and that may be why she's not interested. I'm hoping that as her muscle strength comes back everywhere else, her desire to drink will increase too.

We had a sweet moment yesterday with her. I took Zoë to the hospital with me, and as she came plodding into Eliza's room, scraping her well-worn flip-flops, Eliza looked up and giggled at the familiar sound. I think she even said, "Zoë." It made me beam; she knows her sister just by the sound of her walk!

Opa (Joel's dad) and my sister are going to take Robin and Zoë to the zoo today. Dean could certainly use a break from the dreary hospital. I'm planning to spend the day with Eliza. I hope my heart can handle it, as I've distanced myself from her to a certain extent. As a sidenote, our car is fixed! It ended up being a loose wire—hmm, strange! Thank God for our friend who knew what to look for!

Biting my lip,
Shannon

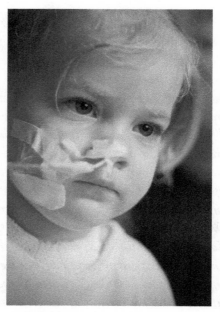

Eliza with feeding tube. © Traina Photography

Robin playing with Eliza who can't sit up on her own.

The Brain

Sent: Monday, October 2, 2006, 5:24 p.m.
Subject: Weary

My heart is still aching today. Our hopes are not shattered, but they are still waning. Unfortunately, Eliza's blood work from this morning showed no change at all in her condition since last week. According to her nephrologist, she needs to be peeing a lot more than she is, about three times more. She said that she's receiving a great amount of fluid through the tube feeding but isn't peeing out as much as is being taken in. However, she has been consistently peeing once a day, even though they're small amounts. This morning she had another wet diaper, but not enough to change her condition.

My head began to spin when a neurologist showed up at her door again today. I thought we were done with that, but her pediatric team has decided it would be wise to go ahead and have an MRI done tomorrow morning to rule out any possible seizure problems. She's still twitching an awful lot—it's getting better, but it's not gone.

I had just returned from asking a question at the nurse's station to see Dean engaged in a conversation with a young doctor. I hadn't seen him before and wondered who he was, but not wanting to interrupt, I continued to listen while I put on my face mask and proceeded to scrub down my hands to *prepare Eliza's dialysis machine for the next round of therapy.*

Dean began asking questions, "What type of brain damage will you be looking for, and what are the potential long-term ramifications?"

The young resident neurologist, not much older than me, began, "Well, there are several scenarios that we can't really play out until we have a complete MRI, but she could be looking at anything from long-term learning difficulties to more severe brain damage."

I tried to choke back my fear as the words slipped from his mouth, but then I couldn't help but recall my own history. Didn't they say I'd never learn well? That I would never graduate out of special ed or go to college? And here I stood, having defied them all? Completing the task of replacing the dialysis solution and beginning the new cycle, I looked over the crib at Eliza, who smiled at me, extending her hand toward me. I gave her a quick pat as I walked around the crib toward the doctor, taking off my face mask. "Well, as her mother…"

The resident did a double take as his eyes grew wide. "You're her mother?" Apparently, he must have thought I was just a nurse, but as he saw me caring for my daughter, his respect seemed to grow.

"Yes, and I think it's probably a good thing we're doing an MRI, although it does make me nervous. I'd like to know what we're looking at long-term, if possible. There are so many therapies out there today that the earlier we know if she has an issue, the sooner we can get her care, right?"

"Yes, I suppose that makes sense. But again, it depends on what we find. We have her slotted for an MRI tomorrow morning, and then we'll have a better idea."

I had to stop myself and think hard about this. I decided it's a good thing to have an MRI. If there is any damage, we can possibly head it off at the pass and get her therapy now. I'm the kid that had really bad dyslexia, speech impediment, and walked into walls (literally) when I was in kindergarten; there were questions as to whether or not I was retarded. I was given all the special help I needed—speech pathology, occupational therapy, and special ed in elementary school through sixth grade—and now, well, I think I'm better off for it. Eliza doesn't have to be any different. It was a rough road, but it's made me who I am today. Eliza may have some challenges ahead, but I'm not giving up on her—my dad taught me that!

After the neurologist left, we were visited by a speech pathologist, who wanted to observe Eliza eating. There are still concerns about her not swallowing much. She still has very little interest in fluids. But I had a glimpse of hope yesterday and on Saturday when she took three to four sips of milk. They were obviously labored, but she did it! Eliza is also getting stronger. She has pulled herself up to standing in her crib, and according to Dean, she sat up in her bed for a whole seven minutes yesterday before falling over. She's holding her head up better too.

As for coming home, we are still waiting. We are hoping the dialysis equipment was ordered today and that it will arrive at our house by next Monday. Once it's here, they will send us home. Currently, they are planning on sending her home with the feeding tube. I'm a bit overwhelmed by that, but I guess we'll figure that out when the time comes. Thankfully, my mom was a registered nurse and can help me with this stuff. But I'm concerned as Eliza has pulled out her feeding tube successfully the past four nights, regardless of how much we tape it to her. She hates it, but so would I!

Our car is still acting up—it's much like Eliza. It's working, then it's not working. It's getting better, then, well, it's acting up again. Maybe they will get better at the same time. Oh, I forgot to mention, Joel got a bad cold yesterday. It has knocked him out pretty good. I was wondering when all this was going to catch up to him. I'm feeling pretty good, just really tired and operating on autopilot.

I wish I could write and say, "She's all better! Peeing great! No more problems!" Maybe sometime soon, but for now, Joel and I are singing along with Dory from Finding Nemo, *"Just keep swimming, just keep swimming..."*

Waiting,
Shannon

First Corinthians 1:25, 27–29 says, "For the foolishness of God is wiser than man's wisdom and the weakness of God is stronger than man's strength.... But God chose the foolish things of this world to shame the wise; God chose the weak things of the world to shame the strong. He chose the lowly things of this world and the despised things and the things that are not to nullify the things that are, so that no one may boast before Him."

Sent: *Thursday, October 5, 2006, 8:03 a.m.*
Subject: *Say it's your birthday...*

It's Robin's birthday too, yeah! I don't have much time today. I've been spending a lot more time at the hospital this week than last. Eliza was scheduled for an MRI on Tuesday, but unfortunately, she didn't respond well to the sedation. She got tired, then really, really loopy—she was cracking herself up, as well as me. I've never seen her like that before. Now I know what a drunken two-year-old looks like. So she was rescheduled for an MRI yesterday morning. It took a ton of medication for her to actually get sedated. She's such a calm baby that the nurses assumed she would go out right away, but she has her own stubborn streak and refused to close her eyes even when they got too heavy to keep open. She kept one little slit of an eye open for ten minutes, reaching up for me. "Mommy, Mommy." But as one of the nurses said with a wink, "We always tend to win in the end."

Once her MRI was done, she pretty much slept the entire day, and I'm hoping she slept through the night for my dad. She slept most of Tuesday as well. I put her down after her failed sedation, and she zonked out, of course for the entire day, after we left the imaging center. Why couldn't she do that when we were there? She doesn't seem to like the "easy" way. The neurologist stuck his head in her room last night to let me know they didn't see anything they didn't want to, but it's apparent the toxins have done some damage. He's coming back this morning to give us a full report, which is why I'm in a hurry.

Eliza's nephrologists have put her on a third blood pressure medicine. She has struggled with high blood pressure since the beginning and will likely continue from here on out. But the night before last, it went down to 94/47 (it's been as high as 165/100 two weeks ago—their goal is keep it below 110/50). My jaw hit the floor—I was so excited! So hopefully they will take her off one of the first two meds. Her doctor had put off putting her on the third medicine since it increases her creatinine levels, messing with her charting of Eliza's kidney function. It will also increase her potassium, which I was told is actually good news at this point.

She has started showing a "tiny" bit more interest in fluids. It's been hard since she's slept much of the past two days, but hopefully today she'll be more alert. We took her to pet therapy last night in the hospital playroom. She got to pet a few beautiful, soft dogs and watch them do tricks. She smiled even though her eyelids were still super heavy.

I have been on my own in terms of the dialysis machine since Tuesday, connecting and disconnecting Eliza, setting up and tearing down the machine. I'm starting to feel more confident about it, and I think I'm finally coming to terms with the fact that this "thing" is coming home with us. Yesterday marked the fourth week since Eliza started throwing up at home. Where has the time gone? We won't get discharged until next Wednesday, but that date seems to continue to change, so we'll see—although we're anxious to have her home!

Joel is still fighting his cold. Today is the girls' birthday, and we're hoping to celebrate with a family meal at the hospital. However, our car, which continued to act up, is at a repair shop. Is there anyone locally who would be able to pick it up for us today? We need it back by tomorrow morning since we're having tires put on it. I didn't tell Joel that I'd ask around, but picking up the car may interfere with his being able to be at our family meal tonight.

I'm off.

Joel with Zoë and Eliza celebrating the twin's birthday

Sent: *Friday, October 6, 2006, 9:20 a.m.*
Subject: *Eliza's brain*

My dad met with the neurologist yesterday, and basically, Eliza has a bilateral signal disruption at the base of her brain. This means her coordination has been disrupted for a while. They believe it's a metabolic disruption rather than a stroke with bleeding and/or hemorrhaging, which is really good news and likely means it's short-term. Signal disruption is causing her to struggle with standing, holding objects, getting food directly to her mouth, etc. All of a sudden, her behavior from last week makes sense to me. Those Shiga toxins hit her hard!

I don't know if this is good news or not, but her nephrologist, who specializes in HUS and pediatric dialysis, said that Eliza is the first patient she's ever had to call for an MRI. She said, "This is new territory for me." The toxins from the E. coli *always attack the major body systems, but Eliza seems to have been hit extra hard. We're hopeful that with time, that part of her brain will heal on its own. I guess there's no set formula or therapy that helps with this type of injury.*

Last night was a ton of work for all of us—coordinating all of us getting to the hospital, getting all the presents and food there, etc. But at the end of the day, I would say it was a success, as Eliza seemed to come alive! She was giggling, playing with balloons, and she even ate a bunch of plain spaghetti, bread, and meat. And to top it off, she was feeding herself! I can't help but wonder how long she's been waiting for us to all be together again—she appeared to be relishing in it.

So we left the hospital exhausted but happy. We are still dealing with jealousy from both Robin and Eliza. They seem to like looking at and watching each other, but they have yet to directly interact. They were both crying quite a bit last night to get my attention. Jealousy is a powerful emotion, and I wonder how long it will take them to "get over it." There's only one mommy to go around, and I love them both!

As I raced out the door, my mom drove me to the auto repair shop to pick up our car. I was in a hurry since the neurologist had requested to speak to me personally during her morning rounds, and I had a tight schedule to keep if I was going to arrive on time. As I went in to speak to our friend and reconcile our bill, he handed me an invoice with a smile. I was starting to dig for my credit card when he said, "No, Shannon. We've got you covered." I looked at him puzzled, and he handed me the car key as he made his way around the desk. "This one's on me." He gave me a side hug and ushered me toward the car. In a hurry and baffled, I muttered, "Are you sure?"

"Go. You have other things that need to be done."

I felt the tears stinging the corner of my eyes. Was he really going to just let me go and not have me pay for our repair? In the midst of so much fire, that would be a cool sip of water. Getting in the driver's seat and pulling out of the parking lot, I ripped open our invoice. Under the "Parts and Labor" description was written, "God has given gifts to each of you from his great variety of spiritual gifts. Manage them well so that God's generosity can flow through you. Are you called to be a speaker? Then speak as though God himself were speaking through you. Are you called to help others? Do it with all the strength and energy that God supplies. Then God will be given glory in everything through Jesus Christ (1 Pet. 4:10–11)."

Lifting my hand to heaven, I wept and gave thanks to the Lord as I sped toward the hospital. I ran the ten-minute walk from the parking garage to Eliza's room just as the neurologist was wrapping up a conversation with my father, only catching the last few minutes of her appointment. We showed her the video we had taken of Eliza batting balloons the night before at her party. She was happily surprised to see the progress already developing in Eliza's coordination. "I believe she's going to recover with time—no guarantees, of course, but given this improvement since I last saw her, it's hard to not imagine a full recovery. I would like to see her continue with physical and occupational therapy, and I'll schedule a clinic follow-up in three to four months." Thank you, Jesus! Another praise today!

My father and I exchanged looks of relief as the neurologist left. "I'm happy to have that out of the way," I offered while scooping Eliza out of the crib. She did look better, more alert somehow. "Let's take her on a walk down the hall today. She could use some 'outside' time."

"I noticed a playroom associated with a clinic farther down the hall into a separate corridor. We could take her down there," my dad offered while cleaning up his breakfast dishes. "She's going to get through this, honey. We just have to be patient. One step at a time. Last week she couldn't sit up unassisted, and today, well, look at her. She has gained a lot more muscle control."

Pulling Eliza in a hospital-issued Red Ryder wagon, we meandered down the hall, waving at the team of nurses bustling around their central desk. We passed Amber's room, waving at her mother, Doris, who we often saw at the coffee machine. Amber was a sixteen-year-old girl who had been admitted days before Eliza with a rare blood disorder. "How you two doing today?" I smiled.

"Fine. Just watching some TV," offered Doris from her corner chair.

"Hi, Eliza! How are you?" Amber smiled as she sat up taller in her bed, beaming in her direction. "Thank you for sharing your birthday balloons with me!" she said, pointing toward the blue and yellow balloons tied to the end of her bed. Amber had been airlifted from a rural hospital, and Doris was staying at the Ronald McDonald House next door, drawing us to them. We wished we could offer them more, knowing they didn't have any local family to help, but their friendship also forced us to be thankful for the minimal twenty-five-minute drive home.

Arriving in the playroom, Eliza perked up, lifting her hands for me to pick her up. To my surprise, she squirmed her way down to the floor. Unsure, I looked at my dad. "Well, I guess we'll see what she can do." I held her fingers as she stood up, uncertain at first, but quickly gaining confidence in her own weight. Eliza put one foot out, wobbling into her first step, then falling. "Dad! Did you see that? She's trying! She wants to walk!" Tears stung at the corner of my eyes as I lifted her up again.

My dad pulled out his cell phone and started filming. "Eliza, come to Peepa. Come here, girl. I know you can do it." Unsteady again, she thrust out her right foot, taking another step, followed by another before falling again. After another few tries, she was up and running from one toy to another—still wobbly, but fully able to get herself around. "Dad, I can't believe it! She's walking again. My baby is walking! Eliza, how does it feel? Your second first steps! And we have you on film!" Overwhelmed, my dad and I exchanged a few tears as things began looking brighter for Eliza. Thank You again, Jesus! I'm overwhelmed by Your goodness and blessings today! You have been so kind and gentle to me today!

Robin, Shannon, Eliza & Zoë © Traina Photography

Later in the afternoon, my joy waned as outside influences began pressing in on my heart. When the enemy senses victory, he attacks from another angle. A visitor who I knew loved Jesus shrugged their shoulders in despair as they were leaving, as if to say, "Oh well, we'll just have to see if God will get you through this." I wanted to weep. Couldn't they see? Didn't they know that God had not left us? How could they not see that? How could they so callously shrug their shoulders at the great works of God? My heart was crushed, not for myself, but for the lack of faith displayed in such a small gesture. O Lord, do Your people really doubt You so much? Why couldn't he have encouraged me toward Your char-

acter and the love we know You have for us? Oh, it hurts, Lord! Wake up Your people! May they know You, really know You, for who you are. May we see you all the more clearly in the midst of this darkness!

"*The degree of hopelessness I have for others comes from never realizing that God has done anything for me. Is my own personal experience such a wonderful realization of God's power and might that I can never have a sense of hopelessness for anyone else I see? Has any spiritual work been accomplished in me at all? The degree of panic activity in my life is equal to the degree of my lack of personal spiritual experience.*"[8] *If God has worked before, why wouldn't or couldn't He work now? And would I trust Him regardless of the outcome?*

Words from a church message a few weeks before flooded my thinking. Our church had been studying through the book of Hebrews, and I smiled as I realized how gently the Lord had been preparing our hearts for this very hour. In Hebrews 3:7–14, the writer warns against unbelief:

"*Today if you hear my voice, do not harden your hearts as you did in the rebellion, during the time of testing in the desert, where your fathers tested and tried me and for forty years saw what I did. That is why I was angry with that generation, and I said, "Their hearts are always going astray, and they have not known my ways, so I declare on oath in my anger, 'They shall never enter my rest.'*

"*See to it, brothers, that none of you has a sinful, unbelieving heart that turns away from the living God. But encourage one another daily, as long as*

8 Oswald Chambers, "The Staggering Question," in *My Utmost for His Highest*, ed. James Reimann (Crewe, United Kingdom: Oswald Chambers Publications Assn., Ltd., 1992). Used with permission by Our Daily Bread Publishing, Grand Rapids MI 49501.

it is called Today, so that none of you may be hard-
ened by sins' deceitfulness. We have come to share in
Christ if we hold firmly till the end the confidence
we had at first."

"Today" is literally today. Are we hearing God
today? Are we looking for Him today? Is it possible
He's working and we're just too busy complaining to
notice? This passage is referring to the Israelites, who
had seen the mighty, miraculous works of God that
freed them from their slavery in Egypt. He had pro-
vided miraculously for them by drawing water from
a rock and manna that fell from heaven, and yet
they continued to whine and complain. And once
they sent spies to look at the promised land, they
allowed the "monsters" and obstacles to overwhelm
them into unbelief that their God would or could
provide for them. They weren't willing to take God
at His word. They didn't trust the promises, which
angered the Lord.

The warning is still ours today. We need to
be careful to not fall into the trap of unbelief that
deceives us into believing God's promises aren't true.
But rather, we are exhorted to encourage one another
daily regarding God's love and precious care for His
children. The afternoon I had my breakdown after
the law appointment, I spoke to my pastor's wife on
the phone. She asked me, "Shannon, what can I do
for you? How can I continue to help you?" I asked
her to not forget to share truth with me. The one
thing I needed from her more than anything was to
keep truth ever before me. I told her, "I need truth,
truth, truth. The enemy is lying to me like crazy
right now, tempting me toward unbelief in God's
promises. Please keep them before me!"

When we were in the midst of great suffering,
we needed to be reminded of God's precious promises.

I needed to remember that "God is not human, that He should lie, not a human being, that He should change His mind. Does He speak and then not act? Does he promise and then not fulfill?" (Num. 23:19). Paul repeats this again in Titus 1:2, "In the hope of eternal life, which God, who does not lie, promised before the beginning of time." God cannot lie, period. We either believe Him and join with the "great cloud of witnesses…running with perseverance the race marked out for us" (Heb. 12:1) or we begin a steady stream of questioning and unbelief that can lead ultimately to our parchment in the wilderness.

The word harden *in Hebrews 3:8 is the Greek word* skleruno, *which refers to the hardening of an object to the point of inflexibility.[9] It's where we get the word* sclerosis. *We have all heard of arteriosclerosis, the hardening of heart arteries that have built up plaque over time. The only known way a doctor can determine if a patient has arteriosclerosis is through a stress test. The same is true of us; the only way we can know the true state of our heart toward the Lord is during times of stress. What is our first reaction? Is it to complain and curse the Lord, or is it to turn to Him for guidance and to hear His voice crying in the wilderness? I was challenged once when a friend asked me, "What is the first word out of your mouth when you stub your toe on a metal cabinet?"*

There are many warnings in Hebrews regarding the care of our heart toward God, but I was struck by two. The first is found in Hebrews 2:1, "We must pay more careful attention therefore, to

---

9   James Strong, *Strong's Concordance: Greek* (Nashville: Thomas Nelson, 2003), 4,645.

what we have heard, so that we do not drift away."
We must keep our hearts from drifting off course like
a ship at sea by paying close attention to what we
have heard and believe about God.

Second warning is in Hebrews 3:12, "See to it,
brothers, that none of you has a sinful, unbelieving
heart that turns away from the living God." How
do we do this? The answer is found in the next verse,
"But encourage one another daily, as long as it is
called Today, so that none of you may be hardened
by sin's deceitfulness." We need one another! For
every Paul there is Timothy, and for every David
there is a Jonathan. We were never meant to walk
this road alone; find fellowship and seek to encour-
age others! Spend time with the Lord daily, seeking
His Word for you today. We cannot live on yester-
day's manna—we have been sustained by it, but
there is fresh food for us today that we're meant to
partake of.

We had such a wide range of responses to our
circumstances. The people that encouraged us the
most were those that continued to point us toward
the character of God. No matter how hurting we
were, they reminded us in love that God would
never leave us and that His love is sure. His works
are unpredictable, but His love is sure. We couldn't
put our faith in Him doing this or that specifically,
like some encouraged, but we could put our faith
in who He is—our Redeemer, Creator, Friend,
Covenant-Keeper, Father, and Savior, the God we
see brought to life through the pages of Scripture.

Blessings and Loving Discipline

Sent: *Friday, October 6, 2006, 11:01 p.m.*
Subject: *She's starting to walk!*

Today was a milestone as Eliza started walking on her own! I have been praying that she would be able to walk out of that hospital rather than have to be carried, and it may just happen! She is still weak, given the condition of her brain; she's a bit wobbly and often needs assistance, but we were thrilled to see her take her first steps. It was just a week and a half ago that we had to hold her head up for her, and she couldn't even sit up unassisted then. My baby is coming back. We also had another family meal there tonight since last night seemed to really boost Eliza's spirits. She loves eating whatever the rest of us are eating, and I think she's starting to feel like a "normal" little girl again. She even started playing with Zoë and Robin tonight, asking to get down on the floor with them.

I learned yesterday from our nephrologist that dialysis only provides 10 percent kidney function! I was shocked! That's why when you're on dialysis, you need a special diet and the like. So I joked with the doctor that Eliza must have, what, 0.5 percent *of her function back right now? She just smiled and said that could be about right.*

A normal child has about five hundred grams of pee per day, and Eliza is slowly increasing in amount each day (hip, hip, hooray!), but it's still under one hundred grams. It's still possible for her to regain a large amount of kidney function, but it may take some time. So we've adjusted and have become comfortable with the idea of bringing the dialysis machine home while her body "wakes up." It's like preparing for another child—where will it sleep? Will it get along with the other children?

Eliza's creatinine levels are still ranging around 4.5–5.0 (normal 0.4–0.9)—still way too high! The doctors will have indication of how well her kidneys function based on the lowering of her creatinine levels, increased pee output, and decreased amount of fluid the dialysis machine is pulling out each night, which would indicate her kidneys have already done the work.

I'm bummed by the reality of our responsibility as parents for Eliza's home care, which seems to increase daily. She's going to require three shots a week, which I'm sure I can handle; I just don't want to! With her special diet, she's going to require a phosphorus binder every four hours, and if she's still tube feeding when she leaves the hospital, it will mean either Joel or I getting up twice a night to administer it. Pray that she would no longer require the tube feeding! I can handle bringing home the dialysis machine, but I really, really don't want to bring home the feeding tube! They are planning to train us next week on how to insert the feeding tube up her nose and down her throat, which is an awful process of forcing it up her nose until she swallows the tube. I know we can do it—I just don't want to.

I want to remain her mother, whom she can run to for comfort, not the nurse inflicting physical pain. That's all there is to it—even I have my limits.

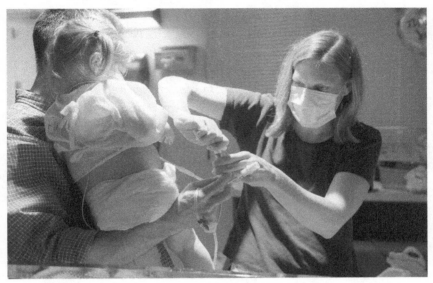

Shannon changing Eliza's dialysis ©Traina Photography

Eliza appears to have just discovered her dialysis catheter tube. She was sitting in her crib yesterday as she began looking at it slowly, inspecting it mentally, in the same way babies inspect their newly discovered belly button. "Is that a part of me? What do I do with it? Where did it come from?"

Because of Eliza's condition, she had been cared for on the oncology ward since leaving the ICU, which opened our eyes to a whole new world of illness and suffering. Baldheaded babies were the norm on our wing, as many came and left after their chemo treatments. There was one last night when we heard a young boy screaming next door from the pain of his chemo—it took several nurses to hold him down as his screams for help drifted through the wall separating our rooms. Oh, Lord, it hurts. So little and yet so much pain, Lord. Comfort him, please!

We heard of an eighteen-year-old girl who had been readmitted across the hall the previous week with terminal cancer. She was very sick and bedridden, and yet she kept insisting to the nursing staff that she would be going home on Monday. The nurses did their best to comfort her and gently remind her of the graveness of her condition—there wasn't any chance she would be going home that soon. However, the girl kept insisting that Jesus had told her she would be going home on Monday, and sure enough, she went home to be with her Savior, Jesus, early this week. She had been right; she would be going home on Monday, just as He had told her. Lord, if it should be Eliza's time, please speak gently to me as You did with this sweet girl. Take me by the hand and lead me. You are the ultimate authority, not the doctors, not me, not the machine or the medicines, but You and You alone. So please, Lord, be gentle with my heart, which You gave me toward Eliza as her mother. I trust that you have drawn me into the desert to speak kindly to me and to Eliza. Give me Your perfect love, which casts out fear since fear has to do with punishment.

The death of this young lady left ripples throughout the nurses' station and encouraged my heart that God really does know all. I had been reminded before that those of us found in Jesus are immortal until God calls us home. He knows our beginning from end, which means we don't have to fret over it. One of my favorite lines from Little Women *came to mind. As one of the sisters, Beth, was lying on her deathbed, she told her dearest sister and friend Jo, "If God is calling me home, there is none who can stand in His way." I held this truth deep in my heart for Eliza. She wouldn't die until God said it was time for her to go, and that was such a comfort. He holds the keys to life and death, and none will stand in His way either in life or death!*

There were moments in the midst of Eliza's deepest pain that I begged Him to take her home. I couldn't stand to see her suffering so deeply, and I knew she would be better off in His arms, but He encouraged my heart to keep coming to Him on her behalf, that she would have life, His life both here and there in eternity. I longed for her to be protected from pain, to make it stop, but if God didn't withhold His own Son from suffering, how could I do any less?

Hebrews 5:7–9 gives us a glimpse, a rare glimpse, into the personal life of Jesus, "During the days of Jesus' life on earth, he offered up prayers and petitions with loud cries and tears to the One who could save Him from death, and He was heard because of His reverent submission. Although He was a Son, He learned obedience from what He suffered and, once made perfect, He became the source of eternal salvation for all who obey Him." If God's own Son lived a life crying out to His Father for help in the midst of His suffering, not just on the cross, but in everyday living, then how much more so do I need to cry out to my Father in the midst of my own struggles? What a beautiful picture and example Jesus is to us in these verses. He learned submission through suffering! Do I really think I can learn submission apart from it? Why do I run from suffering when it holds such rich hope in following Jesus? That I may learn to be obedient and submissive to the only One worth living for!

"Therefore, since we have a great high priest who has gone through the heavens, Jesus the Son of God, let us hold firmly to the faith we profess. For we do not have a high priest who is unable to sympathize with our weaknesses, but we have one who has been tempted in every way, just as we are—yet was without sin. Let us then approach the throne of grace with confidence, so that we may receive mercy and find grace to help us in our time of need" (Heb. 4:14–16).

Jesus set an example for us of approaching the throne of grace. He didn't require mercy from His Father since He never sinned, but He sure needed God's grace to help Him overcome, as is pictured in the Hebrews 5 verses. He was tempted in every way yet was without sin. I've heard these verses explained in relation to mountain climbing. Once we've accepted Jesus as our Lord and Savior, having professed our sinful state and need for salvation, God gives us His Spirit and word as equipment to begin our mountain climb toward knowing Jesus better, our sanctification. There will be many times in our journey when we slip and fall, losing our grip and tumbling back to the base of the mountain. But not all hope is lost! This is when God sends us His ambulance of mercy—the gift of forgiveness and cleansing from our wrongdoing. We receive the beautiful gift of not receiving the just punishment we deserve for our sin as He cleanses our self-inflicted wounds and sends us back to the mountain. As we continue to climb, we begin to learn how to "find grace to help us in our time of need" (Heb. 4:16). When we begin to feel ourselves slipping, we can call out to God for help, and in His grace, an unmerited favor, He will reach down and help us climb. He will help us to overcome our greatest barriers as we cry out for His help! We need His grace to overcome. Jesus's life was a living example of one overcoming through the power of God's grace. Jesus didn't overcome sin by using His God powers; He was fully man, like us. He showed us how to walk with the Father in continual grace! The question these verses beg us to answer in retrospect is, Am I seeking to live in God's mercy or grace? Do I desire to overcome through God's grace, or am I content to live in His mercy?

"We…plead with you not to receive the grace of God in vain" (2 Cor. 6:1). The grace you had yesterday will not be sufficient for today. Grace is the overflowing favor of God, and you can always count on it being available to draw upon as needed. "In much patience, in tribulations, in needs, in distresses"—that is where our patience is tested (6:4). Are you failing to rely on the grace of God there? Are you saying to yourself, "Oh well, I won't count this time"? It is not a question of praying and asking God to help you; it is taking the grace of God now. We tend to make prayer the preparation for our service, yet it is never that in the Bible. Prayer is the practice of drawing on the grace of God. Don't say, "I will endure this until I can get away and pray." "Pray now—draw on the grace of God in your moment of need. Prayer is the most normal and useful thing; it is not simply a reflex action to your devotion to God. We are very slow to learn to draw on God's grace for prayer."[10]

"The Father knows the things you have need of before you ask Him" (Matt. 6:8). Then why should we ask? The point of prayer is not to get answers

---

[10] Oswald Chambers, "Drawing on the Grace of God—Now, June 26th," in *My Utmost for His Highest*, ed. James Reimann, (Crewe, United Kingdom: Oswald Chambers Publications Assn., Ltd., 1992). Used by permission of Our Daily Bread Publishing, Grand Rapids MI 49501.

from God but to have perfect and complete one-ness with Him. If we pray only because we want answers, we will become irritated and angry with God. We receive an answer every time we pray, but it does not always come in the way we expect, and our spiritual irritation shows our refusal to identify ourselves truly with our Lord in prayer. We are not here to prove that God answers prayer, but to be living trophies of God's grace."[11]

Sent: *Sunday, October 8, 2006, 10:07 p.m.*
Subject: *The latest from Joel*

Joel here. A week ago, our pastor asked if there was anything we needed. Since we had food covered for the next two weeks and he seemed to want for there to be something to help with, I said, "Well, we do need new tires for our car." He e-mailed, saying, "Joel, maybe a little bit of brightness in your clouds. The Lord has a set of tires for your car."

I replied with, "That sounds too good to be true! Now, when I said we 'needed' tires for our car, I didn't mean that we couldn't pay for them—I just meant that there was one more thing on top of all this that 'needed' to be done, so I hope that we can pay for them at least."

We spoke later, and he said he already had the set of tires in his car, so we just needed to find a time to install them. He also voiced my wishes to the "tire donor," and "they" replied that they wanted to help our family out, so this was how they were doing it!

---

[11] Oswald Chambers, "The Cross in Prayer, August 6th," in *My Utmost for His Highest*, ed. James Reimann (Crewe, United Kingdom: Oswald Chambers Publications Assn., Ltd., 1992). Used with permission by Our Daily Bread Publishing, Grand Rapids MI 49501.

So thank God for whoever set us up with new tires! And thank you to our friend who fixed our car ignition problem for free as a way to bless us.

On to more blessings: Eliza slept very well Saturday night after eating a whole *plain hamburger. Because she slept well, I slept well too. We had a great day of laughing, tickling, smiles, playing, some more walking, and a good afternoon nap. Thanks so much to my work for providing even more balloons (for the twins' birthday last Thursday)! Eliza loves pointing to them, saying, "Ba-oo, ba-oo!" And that's where the fun begins. She hits them and giggles and grabs and bats and smiles and laughs— great fun for all and a sweet reprieve from the reality of her illness.*

One of our nephrologists (on call on the weekends) came in this evening when Shannon and I were both at the hospital for his daily rounds. We knew he went to church, because his rounds are usually in the morning, but all the nurses say, "He'll come around later, because he always does Sunday rounds after church." So in our conversation, he saw that we are Christians, and he prayed a wonderful prayer with us for Eliza. He squeezed my hand so tight against my ring that it hurt, but the prayer was honest, heartfelt, praising Jesus Christ and God the Father, full of scripture and blessing, asking for specific healing of her metabolism, cells, blood, and kidneys in terms that only doctors (and God) fully understand. Amen!

We will more than likely come home this Thursday—that's when all the dialysis equipment will be here. Shannon's doing a great job of rear-

*ranging clothes and closets to make everything ready
for her homecoming. We can hardly wait.*

> *Yours by the prayers of the saints
> (all you who are in Christ Jesus),
> Joel*

Tested

Sundays were important days for me, as I longed to be with the fellowship of believers at our church, worshipping the Lord among them. I hardly ever made it past the first worship song before I was a mess of tears, but my heart connected with the Lord in deep ways through singing. Most mornings before I left for the hospital, I would listen to my favorite worship songs while showering, pouring my heart out with loud tears before the Lord. It was always very healing to empty myself before Him, and I always sensed His meeting me in that place. God sees and hears our moments of great desperation; in fact, I think He longs for them.

One of my greatest heroes of the faith is found in Matthew 15:21–28, the account of the Canaanite woman approaching Jesus in utter desperation: "Jesus withdrew to the region of Tyre and Sidon. A Canaanite woman from that vicinity came to him, crying out, 'Lord, Son of David, have mercy on me! My daughter is suffering terribly from demon-possession.' The Canaanites were arch enemies of the Jews—considered unclean, gentiles, in the Jewish tradition, not worthy of consideration. So, the audacity and boldness of this woman to approach Jesus and the disciples, crying out for their attention is unthinkable. And not only that, but she's daring to call Jesus, 'Lord, Son of David!' Who is she to make such claims?! He could never be her Lord! He is the Lord of the Jews, having come from the line of David and yet here she is, crying out for HIS mercy! How dumbfounded the disciples must have been at her determination.

"Jesus did not answer a word. So his disciples came to him and urged him, 'Send her away, for she keeps crying out after us.' Apparently, they were embarrassed and annoyed by this woman and the scene she's created. They want Jesus to send her away; after all,

He's not addressing her either, showing no interest in wanting contact with her, an unclean gentile. He answered (apparently addressing the disciples), 'I was sent only to the lost sheep of Israel.'

"The woman came and knelt before Him. 'Lord, help me!' she said."

The Greek word for *knelt* in this passage is *proskuneó*, which means to kiss the ground when prostrating before a superior, to *worship*, ready "to fall down/prostrate oneself to adore on one's knees."[12] She, a gentile woman, had fallen on the ground in outright humility and desperation before the man she had claimed in her heart to be the Lord over all things!

I find it significant that she acknowledged her daughter's demon possession, showing a level of insight into the spiritual realm. Here we find her prostrate, showing great faith and acknowledgment toward Jesus's reign over the spiritual world—she must have held a deep belief that He had the power to suppress even the darkest of demons. She was living in a notoriously pagan city that had become a commercially magnificent source of cultural and religious seductiveness since the time of Jezebel. Within her grasp were several pagan temples offering a wide range of healing remedies and idol worship, and yet here we find her prostrate at Jesus's feet, worshipping Him in humility and desperation, willingly forsaking the pagan land of her ancestors.

"Jesus [He] replied, 'It is not right to take the children's bread and toss it to their dogs.'"

Jewish rabbis often referred to the gentiles as dogs, using the Greek word *kuón*, meaning scavenging canine (figuratively), a spiritual predator who feeds off others. They viewed the gentiles as unclean, scavenging dogs that were universally despised in the Eastern culture.[13] So it's of great significance that Jesus uses the word *kunariois*, which refers to a household pet or puppy that is cared for. I'm sure the Canaanite woman was surprised by Jesus's use of the word

---

[12] James Strong, *Strong's Greek Concordance* (Nashville: Thomas Nelson, 2003), 4,352, http://concordances.org/greek/4352.htm.

[13] James Strong, *Strong's Greek Concordance* (Nashville: Thomas Nelson, 2003), 2,965, http://concordances.org/greek/2965.htm.

puppy in lieu of *scavenger*, which she may have been called before and willingly risked again now. With a gentle tone to His words, I've always pictured a gleam of affection in Jesus's eye, almost daring her to continue coming. He had come for the lost sheep of Israel, but the love for the puppies at His table was not lost.

"Yes, Lord," she said, "but even the dogs [puppies or household pet] eat the crumbs that fall from their mater's table." What boldness! Desperate people do desperate things. She had come to Jesus as herself, a broken gentile mother, seeking His mercy and grace. She acknowledged her need for Him and His ultimate authority and power. She wasn't caught in tradition—there is none in times of desperation, just humility and spiritual nakedness. She fell at His feet, worshipping and pleading!

"Then Jesus answered, 'Woman, you have great faith! Your request is granted.' And her daughter was healed from that very hour."

She was a living example of the verse "Blessed are the poor [beggars] in spirit for theirs is the kingdom of heaven" (Matt. 5:3).

Lord, help me! I fall at Your feet, worshipping You with tears, crying out for my daughter. Have mercy on her, Lord, please! It's not about me; it's all about You. I come to You naked and poor, having nothing to offer you but myself. I lay my rights to self on the altar, trusting You. I know You have the ultimate authority and can heal Eliza with just one word from Your lips, but I also know You work all things for the good of those who love You and choose to throw themselves at the mercy of Your will. She's Yours, I'm Yours, all things are Yours, and I commit them to Your care. Even though I hear little from You right now, I'll continue coming, Lord, until You acknowledge me as You did this Canaanite woman. Give me Your crumbs, Lord! I'll take whatever You are willing to give; just don't turn Your face from me, please.

Eliza, Joel, Zoë, Shannon & Robin © Traina Photography

Shannon and her father, Richard at Children's
Hospital. © Traina Photography

Sent*: Tuesday, October 10, 2006, 2:34 p.m.*
Subject*: Boxes, boxes, and more boxes*

Eliza's peritoneal dialysis equipment has arrived—thirty-nine boxes' worth! I cleared out most of the twins' closet, but they surely won't all fit, so back to the drawing board. Perhaps they will remain lining the hallway between the girls' bedrooms until they get used. We are now waiting for the "machine"—it is being shipped directly to the hospital so the nurses can program it appropriately for Eliza. We were hoping to get discharged on Thursday, but...

Eliza's blood draws the past two days indicate that her dialysis has not been working very efficiently. She has steadily declined since last Friday, which is forcing them to continue playing with her dialysis solution concentration. I was feeling pretty good that she started on the weakest solution available, but today, they are moving her up to the strongest and increasing the time from nine hours a day to twelve in hopes of improving her creatinine and phosphorus levels. If her blood work does not show improvement, she may have to be switched to the other form of dialysis, hemo, which is much, much harder on her system. This morning she threw up, and I know she hasn't felt too good the past few days. Given this, I wonder if they will delay her coming home until next week. I'm very torn; I want her home so we can all be together again (yesterday marked week 4 in the hospital), but I don't want to bring home a really sick child. I realize she's going to be sick either way; I just want her to be as stable as possible.

I want to mention more about our time with her on-call doctor from Sunday. He's a tall black man from Nigeria with a thick accent. He has always intimidated me with his stature and strong presence. Our first encounter with him was the very first night we arrived at Children's via the ambulance. The driver wheeled us into the ER, and as Eliza was being transferred to another gurney, this doctor literally swooped in from nowhere, picked her up in his big hands, and carried her limp body upstairs to the ICU, with a train of us following behind like stunned sheep. We had no idea who he was at that time, but I suppose he had spoken with Eliza's pediatrician on the phone before we arrived. Now that I know him better, I imagine him silently praying over her as we walked up to the ICU. He told us on Sunday that he had been praying for her since she arrived.

I was greatly encouraged to hear him say, "As doctors, we have to give you statistics regarding these cases, but I personally have never had a patient with this syndrome remain on long-term dialysis, and I don't see any reason Eliza has to be an exception. However, there is nothing more we can do for her now but manage her dialysis—it's entirely in God's hands. Pray, pray, pray. God is bigger than any statistics." And man did he pray—such a simple but meaningful prayer! He prayed that God would restore our joy, and boy do I need that! I need the ability more than ever to walk by faith and not by sight; things change every day, and Eliza seems to fluctuate between doing well and struggling, but I need to not focus on the waves around me.

I'm clinging to 1 Peter 1:6–9, "In this you greatly rejoice, though now for a little while you may have had to suffer grief in all kinds of trails. These have come so that your faith—of greater worth than gold, which perishes even though refined by fire—may be proved genuine and may result in praise, glory and honor when Jesus Christ is revealed. Though you have not seen him, you love him; and even though you do not see him now, you believe in him and are filled with an inexpressible and glorious joy, for you are receiving the goal of your faith, the salvation of your souls." God loves me enough to allow this in my life so that I may stand refined before Him.

During a quiet moment at the hospital, as I was crying and feeling defeated, the Lord gently reminded me, "Shannon, you're not the one defeated—the enemy is. I crushed him, remember? You have a choice to make. You can either continue to feel defeated and fall for the lies of the enemy, or you can choose to rejoice and trust Me." Right then and there, I made my choice. I stood up and began to dance around Eliza's crib with such unexplainable joy! I was dancing with the angels that surround her. They never stopped dancing—I did. The angels are forever before the Father in heaven, crying, "Holy, holy, holy is the Lord God Almighty, who was, and is, and is to come" (Rev. 4:8). No matter what is happening here on earth, this fact still remains. He is holy and will remain so forever! Nothing can defeat us or God; He has already won. For those of us found in Jesus, this world is the worst it will ever get for us. Heaven waits.

Pray that I would continue to dance. If you don't know this Savior of mine, my prayer is that one day you will dance as I have danced. There are no words to express the freedom that comes from knowing Jesus, even at times like these. I long and desire for everyone to know, taste, and see what I have seen over the past two decades. My Jesus is real, and He's too good to keep to myself. For those of you who do know my Savior, we are already seated *in the heavenlies with Jesus (Eph. 2:6). Once you accepted Him into your life, you were seated next to Him, where there is nothing that the enemy can do to remove you from that place! Praise Jesus, we have already overcome!*

In Matthew 6:45–52, after feeding the five thousand, we see Jesus ushering the twelve disciples into a boat to go before Him to the other side, to Bethsaida, while He dismissed the crowd. *"After leaving them, he went up on a mountainside to pray. When evening came, the boat was in the middle of the lake, and he was alone on land. He saw the disciples straining at the oars, because the wind was against them. About the fourth watch of the night (between three and six o'clock in the morning) he went out to them, but when they saw him walking on the lake, they thought he was a ghost. They cried out, because they all saw him and were terrified.*

"Immediately he spoke to them and said, 'Take courage! It is I. Don't be afraid.' Then he climbed into the boat with them, and the wind died down. They were completely amazed."

Jesus purposely put the disciples in the boat, knowing the seas might be rough as He went up the mountainside to pray. He was able to see the disciples straining against the oars. So often we have a hard time believing God ushers us into a boat that will weather storms. We naively believe that once we're on "Jesus's team," we will have smooth waters until we're gently roared into heaven. This wasn't the case with His most intimate twelve disciples, so why would it be true of us?

However, did you notice where Jesus was during this storm? He was up on the mountainside, watching and praying! Were the disciples ever really beyond His reach or care as they fought against the *massive waves? Not at all! And neither are we. At any given moment, Jesus may appear in the midst of our greatest trials, calming the waves that threaten to crush us. Until He does appear, trust He is on the mountain, watching your every move, praying for you! And when He determines it's time to come off the mountain, He will command the waves to be still and immediately take you to the desired destination.*

Are we looking for Him in the midst of the storm, or are we too busy straining at the oars, believing our survival will come from our own strength to endure? Keeping above the waves may be necessary, but it's not our only hope. There is one greater than any wave or storm known to man.

Matthew's account of the same events sheds fresh insight, as there was one who was watching: Peter! "Immediately Jesus said to them, 'Take courage! It is I. Don't be afraid.'

"'Lord, if it's you,' Peter replied, 'tell me to come to you on the water.'

"'Come,' he said.

"Then Peter got down out of the boat, walked on the water and came toward Jesus. But when he saw the wind, he was afraid and, beginning to sink, cried out, 'Lord, save me!'

"Immediately Jesus reached out his hand and caught him, 'You of little faith,' he said, 'why did you doubt?'

"And when they climbed into the boat, the wind died down. Then those who were in the boat worshiped him, saying, 'Truly you are the Son of God.'"

Are the storms we face not designed to have the same effect? Aren't they ultimately designed to bring us to the same place where we can say wholeheart-

edly, "Truly you are the Son of God," as we see He is the only one who can save? And the courageous among us may even step out of the boat to meet our Lord, walking on the very waves that caused the hearts of men to fear.

"God does not promise to keep His child immune from trouble; He promises, 'I will be with him in trouble'" (Ps. 91:15). It doesn't matter how real or intense the adversities may be; nothing can ever separate him from his relationship to God. "In all things we are more than conquerors" (Rom. 8:37). Paul was not referring here to imaginary things, but to things that are dangerously real. Either Jesus Christ is a deceiver, having deceived even Paul, or else some extraordinary thing happens to someone who holds on to the love of God when the odds are totally against him. Logic is silenced in the face of each of these things that come against him. Only one thing can account for it—the love of God in Christ Jesus. "Out of the wreck I rise every time."[14]

Sent: *Friday, October 13, 2006, 10:33 a.m.*
Subject: *Confusion*

Everyone's baffled. Why is Eliza not getting better? Why are her numbers still so bad? As you have probably already figured, Eliza is staying put for some time. If I had to guess, I'd say one to two more weeks. We need to see her blood levels improve! The doctors are trying a new strategy; they put Eliza on twenty-four-hour dialysis on Wednesday afternoon. By yesterday morning, her numbers had not

---

[14] Oswald Chambers, "Out of the Wreck I Rise," in *My Utmost for His Highest*, ed. James Reimann (Crewe, United Kingdom: Oswald Chambers Publications Assn., Ltd., 1992). Used with permission by Our Daily Bread Publishing, Grand Rapids MI 49501.

improved, and she looked very dehydrated. Her eyes were sunken into her head, and she doesn't look like herself, which means the dialysis is drawing out too much fluid from her body. So yesterday afternoon, they changed the solution again to try to give her more fluid retention. She has not peed in the past two days, but I'm not surprised since her body is trying to reserve fluid. The doctors are frustrated and confused. She was doing well, so why did her body start rejecting the dialysis? Her creatinine levels are through the roof at 6.1 (normal 0.4–0.9) on Wednesday, and still only at 5.9 yesterday. This may be why she's been throwing up a lot and appears quite weak—too much waste in her body! She's also tethered to her bed now by being connected to the machine all the time—no more trips to the play-room. Because she's on the smallest-size tubing, they don't have any extensions to give her more than five-foot mobility. Poor baby!

The other confusion is her phosphorus levels. They are extremely high, and yet the only way you get phosphorus is through digesting food—she's not eating, so why does she have high numbers? The Nepro shake (Ensure shake specifically for dialysis patients) is all she's eating through her feeding tube. It does have small amounts of phosphorus, but certainly not enough to justify her high numbers. Plus, she's just been throwing it up, anyway, so it shouldn't matter, as far as I'm concerned. Strange, strange, strange.

Her blood pressure is another interesting factor. Two weeks ago, it was still too high, requiring them to put her on a third medication. Yesterday it was way too low! She got down to 67/37, causing the blood pressure machine to set off all sorts of alarms (they want to keep her around 100/50). So they took her off one of the medications to try to increase it. Before last night, it was 80/42—better! But my dad just called and told me he was up most of the night since her blood pressure was in the sixties and she was throwing up all night.

Yesterday was a very hard day for me on many levels. Not only were we getting bad reports on Eliza, but they also called for a code blue on our floor.

The alarm was announced over the loudspeaker with such a calm, uniform manner, "Code blue, code blue, room 3160." It could have been taken for a call for free hamburgers in the lounge. After a few minutes, I heard a rustling outside Eliza's door, and needing more ice, I poked my head into the hallway. Training nurses and hospital staff were scurrying up and down the hall like a family of ants, speaking in hushed tones over their central station. Most of them I'd never seen before. Stepping out and navigating my way past many of them, I walked toward the snack room still puzzled by all the commotion. I edged along the wall, trying to stay out of the way, following my curiosity. As I drew closer to the hub of activity, it slowly began to dawn on me which room was 3160—Amber's! Oh, Lord, not sweet Amber! I had found the anthill, as her room was crowded with equipment and staff. Daring a peek, I saw through the mass of scrubs the familiar paddles of a defibrillator. "Clear!"

Turning away, I bolted into the snack room, all too eager to fill my water cup, which was why I had ventured out in the first place, right? Right, I had a mission, a reason for being here—I needed water. You need water, Shannon. Get your water. *After fumbling with the paper cups and accomplishing my mission, I braved the hall again. Almost bumping into my favorite nurse, I asked in a desperate, hushed whisper, "What's going on?"*

Looking past me toward Amber's door, she offered sadly, "She's not good. They're having to resuscitate her." Doris. Where's Doris? *Immediately, without thought, I turned deeper into the surrounding staff in search of Amber's mother. I could hear her cries, but where was she?* I have to find her! She doesn't have anyone! Hold her, Jesus! Please hold her!

Directly across from Amber's room, in an empty patient room, I found Doris sitting limply on the bed, surrounded by doctors holding her hands and rubbing her back. She was weeping uncontrollably, reaching toward Amber's room; the staff kept her from falling to the ground. I looked deep into her eyes. I know she saw me as she reached again, but one look from the staff told me I must be in the wrong place. I smiled at her weakly, willing her to know how much I cared for her as we locked eyes. Seeing myself in her broken eyes, I began shaking uncontrollably.

Turning, I practically ran back to Eliza's room, passing the nurses' station, shaking so badly the water in my cup was sloshing on the floor. That could be me. That could be Eliza. O Lord, O Lord, make it stop! *Seeing my fear, a few nurses followed me into Eliza's room and tried to distract me with small talk, but it was too late. I had already withdrawn into myself and locked the door. "Just tell me, did she make it?"*

Putting an arm around my shoulder, the nurse led me to a chair. "Yes, she's been transferred upstairs to ICU." The tears came, and I couldn't make them stop as I watched Eliza sleeping in her crib.

In the wee hours the following morning, Amber passed away as the ICU staff tried in vain

*to resuscitate her again. I didn't discover her pass-
ing until after arriving at the hospital and asking
the nursing staff. As soon as I heard, I ran upstairs
in search of her mother, Doris. I walked past the
glass doors of Amber's ICU room, where she had
been lying motionless the day before, two curtains
down from Eliza's ICU cubicle. My stomach sank as
nausea threatened to escape.* Stay calm, Shannon.
Find Doris. *I wandered the halls, figuring she had
to be around somewhere close. I finally asked one of
the staff, who pointed toward a closed office door. I
stood holding the door handle for several minutes,
willing myself to go inside, but also fearful of what I
might find. It was a door we hadn't opened, but one
that played at the edge of our thinking.*

*Steeling my nerves, I cracked it and peered
in. I was immediately seen by a man sitting next
to Doris at a small conference table. She was crying
on the phone, her head in her hands. At the sound
of the door, she looked up but didn't stop talking.
Her bloodshot eyes met mine once again, and we
implored each other for the last time, one hurting
mother to another. Waving at the man sitting next
to her, I closed the door. My heart broke all over
again. As much as I longed to speak with Doris and
hug her before she left, I never saw her again. The
thought of her packing Amber's things and leaving
the hospital alone was more than I could handle.*

*Anger and hurt began to rise in my chest. I
spent the next hour wandering the many intercon-
nected hospital halls, thinking, crying, and praying.
A nurse from Eliza's floor finally caught up to me at
the drinking fountain on the main floor. Knowing
how hard this death had been on us, and out of concern, she had come in search of me.* "Shannon, are
you all right?" *Surprised, I stepped back from her. I*

was happy to remain in my own thoughts, distant from everyone else, but I found myself talking anyway. "I saw Doris. She was crying on the phone. I saw them cleaning Amber's room."

Those probing eyes—she wouldn't stop looking at me with those eyes of compassion and concern. I wanted to run from them, only because I knew they came from working in a place where they are so heavily required. How many times have I seen that look in the past month? Has it changed anything? Is Eliza any better? Is Amber still living? And yet there it is again, that look, one that comes from deep concern and a desire to help. Crushed under the weight of it, I snapped, "How can you work here? How can you see so many children sick and dying and still come to work?"

Taken aback and drawing a deep breath, she muttered, "Because there are many more that we do get to see go home well. Do we overlook those because we've lost some? We hope and work toward the same outcome for every child."

Tearing up, I could feel my heart begin to soften toward her compassion. How many times had I seen her lovingly care for Eliza? She was a gift, a messenger from God to care for these little ones; how could I have lost sight of that and not appreciate it? Seeing her with fresh vision, I hugged her in gratitude, thankful for her and the entire hospital staff. Oh, Lord, how could I have forgotten that you are the master of the outcome? You hold all things in Your hands, not the staff. They are Your instruments, and You've used them in such beautiful ways. Amber is Yours; she is with You now. And if Eliza should go in the same manner, she will be with You as well. Fear not. I have not left You. Forgive me. Help me to see as You do. Help me to love as You do.

My dad said that Eliza's doctor came in this morning to let him know that her blood work looks a smidgen better this morning. Nothing huge, but we'll take whatever we can get. Her phosphorus levels are a bit better too, but she'd like to see more improvement there. Her creatinine is 5.8. They are going to put her through the weekend on twenty-four-hour dialysis in hopes of seeing improvement. If she hasn't improved by Monday, they are going to do a second surgery to put in a hemodialysis port in her forearm. I really, really don't want her to have to undergo hemodialysis—it's much harder on your system than peritoneal. It draws out all your blood and cycles it through a cleansing machine. It takes three hours to cycle. If we had to go this route, she would have to come to the hospital four times a week for three hours of dialysis, and her diet would be even stricter than it already is. I know her doctors don't want to go this route either, but if it means keeping Eliza alive, then what choice do we have?

Our doctor also reminded Dad that at the beginning of all this, she told us it was going to be a long, rough road to getting Eliza well again. We had no idea what she meant at that time—we thought two weeks was a long road, then we thought four weeks was a long road. How long is this road?

I'm sad I don't have more happy news. I wish I could tell you that our life was grand. In fact, I've put off writing the past two days, hoping something better would come along, but in a Pollyanna way, I'll say, "There's always tomorrow." There is no hopelessness with God. Tears, yes, but hopelessness? No. I remind myself of this hourly.

Worshipping with tears!

*****

Sent: *Saturday, October 14, 2006, 3:56 p.m.*
Subject: *Some answers*

Eliza's creatinine didn't change any this morning. Her phosphorus levels are down some, so that's good. The doctor gave Joel a better idea of their synopsis of what is happening with Eliza's body. She is on peritoneal dialysis, which means they inserted a catheter tube into her lower abdomen that fills her peritoneal cavity with a dextrose solution that deflects her blood cells but attracts the waste products in her blood. It basically functions as her kidneys should. But they have been pumping her full of a lot of fluid, which has caused her peritoneum to become inflamed and not function as well as it should. I wish it were as easy as stopping the dialysis to give it a break in order to recover, but without the dialysis, she would, you know, not do well. They have also determined that her body is not processing food as well as it should. She went two weeks without eating anything, and her body is still trying to figure out what to do with food—this may be why she is throwing up so much. She tends to throw up the most during the "fill" cycle of the dialysis when she is being blown up like a balloon. The doctor is going to try to put her on a medicine that should help her digest food better.

So it's looking more and more likely that Eliza will be put on hemodialysis on Monday. They will insert a port tube below her collarbone. She's too little right now for a port in her forearm, which is more typical. Joel asked about the possibility of her ever going back on peritoneal dialysis, and the doctor said he hopes so. He is hoping that Eliza will be able to do peritoneal from home and then come in once a week for hemo to clear out whatever is remaining. But this may be dependent upon our insurance company. Most insurance companies will not cover more than one form of dialysis. But we'll cross that bridge when we get there. Eliza does qualify for Medicare, so maybe between the two it will work out?

I'm trying not to freak out about this next tidbit of information, but it is what it is. The nephrologist still believes that since Eliza has gone so long without recovering more kidney function, she may not recover much more than she already has (have we not heard that before already?). He has suggested that we go ahead and get her name on the list of patients waiting for kidneys. It can take a long time to get a kidney, and he said he'd rather us be ready to go if that should end up being the case. Joel told me to look at this as if we are preparing for a possible tornado. It's like storing canned food on the off chance we should be hit—it doesn't mean we will be, but we're prepared.

My mom and I just went to see Facing the Giants—*I highly recommend it! Wow! It was just the encouragement I needed.*

Waiting,
Shannon

"Since ancient times no one has heard, no ear has perceived, no eye has seen any God besides you, who acts on behalf of those who wait for him" (Isa. 64:4).

As the lights went out in the movie theater, my heart sank. *My baby is in the hospital, fighting for her life, and I'm here, watching a movie. Is this okay? I should be with her, Lord, but everyone thinks a break would be wise right now. Heal her, please, Father! I pray she doesn't have to switch to hemo. Please, please have mercy. Hold her now. Quiet my heart. Give me peace.*

As the movie plot began to build before me, I was caught in rapt attention as the discombobulated young football team struggled to work together in unity. They needed a leader, someone to draw them out of their melancholy, as their coach lamented, "Your attitude is like the aroma of your heart. If your attitude stinks, it means your heart isn't right."

In response to the players' smirks, he drew them to the goal line for the death crawl. Working together, one player crawled on their hands and feet, carrying a teammate on their back to the ten-yard line. "No knees on the ground! Keep your knees off the ground! Show me something! Come on! Let's go! To the ten-yard line!"

Huddling back together as a team, a player asked, "Coach, how strong is our main contender this year?"

"A lot stronger than we are." A teammate smirked.

Hiding his disappointment, the coach retorted, "You've already written our game night off as a loss, Brock?"

"Well, I wouldn't if I knew we could beat them."

"Come here, Brock. You too, Jeremy. I want to see you do the death crawl again, except I want to see your absolute best."

Walking to the goal line as his the team chuckled, Brock asked, "How far do you want me to go? To the thirty-yard line?"

"I think you can get to the fifty-yard line."

"The fifty? I can maybe go to the fifty if no one is on my back."

"I think you can do it with Jeremy on your back, but even if you can't, I want you to promise me you're going to try to give your best."

"All right."

"Your best."

"Okay."

"One more thing," the coach said, pulling out a handkerchief and tying it around Brock's head. "I want you to do it blindfolded."

"Why?"

"Because I don't want you giving up at a certain point when you can go farther. Get down. Jeremy, get on his back. Get a good, tight hold, Jeremy. All right, let's go, Brock. Keep your knees off the ground, just your hands and feet."

Brock's teammates started to watch him with amusement as he headed toward the five-yard line. "A little bit left…all right…show me some good effort," encouraged the coach, walking beside him. "That a way, Brock. Keep coming…that's a good start." As he crossed the twenty-yard line, his teammates showed a bit more attention from the sideline. "There you go, Brock! Good strength," the coach said as he made his way to the thirty-yard line. "That's it, Brock, that's it!"

Struggling toward the forty-yard line, "Am I at the twenty yet?"

"Forget the twenty. You give me your best. You keep going. That's it!" Brock began slowing down and appeared to be slipping at the fifty-yard line. "Now, don't stop, Brock. You have more in you than that."

"I'm not done, just resting a second."

"You need to keep moving. Don't quit until you got nothing left. There you go, keep moving." Brock's teammates became quiet as he edged past the sixty-yard mark, watching with rapt attention.

"Keep moving, Brock. That's it, you keep driving it. Keep your knees off the ground. Keep driving it! Your very best! I want your very best!" Brock kept inching forward over the seventy, then the eighty-yard mark as his coach became louder. "Keep going, keep driving it! Your very best, keep driving it!" His teammates began standing one by one, trailing behind in awe of Brock's advancement. "Keep driving, keep moving! There you go! That's it, you keep driving it! Keep your knees off the ground! Don't quit until you got nothing left! I want everything you got!"

Tears began to run down my face as Brock cried in pain, "It hurts!"

"Don't quit on me! Your very best! Keep driving!"

"He's heavy!"

Getting down at his level, Brock's coach didn't let up as they inched near the ninety-yard line. "I know he's heavy."

"But I'm out of strength!"

"Then negotiate with your body to find more strength, but don't you give up. You keep going, you hear me? You keep going! You're doing good. Do not quit on me! You keep going!"

"It hurts!"

"I know it hurts. You keep going! It's all heart from here! Twenty more steps. You keep going, Brock! Come on! Keep going!"

"It burns!"

"Then let it burn!"

"My arms are burning!"

"It's all heart! You keep going, Brock! Come on! You keep going! You promised me your best! Don't stop, keep going!"

"It's too hard!"

"It's not too hard! You keep going! Come on, Brock, give me more! Keep going, Brock, twenty more steps! Keep going! Give me your best!"

Grunting, Brock continued laboriously toward the end zone. "Don't quit, Brock! Don't quit! Don't you quit!"

"I can't do it!"

"You can! You can! Five more steps, Brock, just five more! Don't quit! Two more! One more!"

Brock collapsed, and Jeremy quickly rolled off his back. Crying, Brock kept his head in the grass. "It's got to be the fifty. It's got to be! I don't have any more."

Lying on the ground, facing him, the coach pulled off his blindfold. "Look up, Brock. You're in the end zone."

As I sat in my theater seat, tears were streaking down my face. *Lord, it hurts! I can't do this! I'm about out of strength! I'm blind and don't know where we're going.* "Don't you quit on Me." *It burns. This is my baby, Lord.* "Give her to Me! You can do this! Don't quit! I'm here! Shannon Schulz, don't you quit on me. Give me your heart! Give her to me!" *It hurts so bad!* "Come on, Shannon, don't quit on Me! You can trust Me." *But I don't know where we're going!* "It's all heart and trust. Give her to Me! Can I count on you to trust Me?" *My legs hurt and are giving out!* "Keep coming! Don't quit! You're doing well. Keep coming!" *It's too hard!* "No, it's not too hard. Just give her to Me! I'm right here. I won't let you go. Shannon, sweet child, endure hardship as discipline. I am treating you as a daughter. For what daughter is not disciplined by her father?"

"If you are not disciplined—and everyone undergoes discipline—then you are an illegitimate child and not a true daughter.

Moreover, you have a human father who disciplined you, and you respected him for it. How much more should you submit to me, the Father of your spirit, and live! Your father disciplined you for a little while as he thought best, but I discipline you for your good, that you may share in *my* holiness. No discipline is pleasant at that time, but painful. Later on, however, it will produce a harvest of righteousness and peace for those who have been trained by it. Therefore, strengthen your feeble arms and weak knees" (Heb. 12:7–12).

Perseverance means more than endurance—more than simply holding on until the end. A saint's life is in the hand of God like a bow and arrow in the hands of an archer. God is aiming at something the saint cannot see, but our Lord continues to stretch and strain, and every once in a while, the saint says, "I can't take any more." Yet God pays no attention; He goes on stretching until His purpose is in sight, and then He lets the arrow fly. Entrust yourself to God's hands. Proclaim as Job did, "Though He slay me, yet will I trust Him" (Job 13:15).

God ventured His all in Jesus Christ to save us, and now He wants us to venture our all with total abandoned confidence in Him. There are areas in our lives where that faith has not worked in us as yet, places still untouched by the life of God. There were none of those places in Jesus Christ's life, and there are to be none in ours. Jesus prayed, "This is eternal life, that they may know You" (John 17:3). The real meaning of eternal life is a life that can face anything it has to face without wavering. If we will take this view, life will become one great romance, a glorious opportunity of seeing wonderful things all the time. God is disciplining us to get us into this central place of power."[15]

Thank You, Lord, that You love me enough to work this faith in my life. You have opened the door of opportunity to trust You deeper. I believe; help me overcome my unbelief! Help me to not throw away my confidence. It will be richly rewarded. Help me persevere so that when I

---

[15] Oswald Chambers, "The Faith to Persevere," in *My Utmost for His Highest*, ed. James Reimann (Crewe, United Kingdom: Oswald Chambers Publications Assn., Ltd., 1992). Used with permission by Our Daily Bread Publishing, Grand Rapids MI 49501.

have done Your will, I can receive what You have promised. For in just a very little while, "You who is coming will come and will not delay; but Your righteous one will live by faith (let that be me!), and if I shrink back, You will not be pleased with me." Help me to not be one of those who shrinks back and are destroyed, but one who believes and is saved (Heb. 10:33–39).

Sent*: Saturday, October 15, 2006, 9:01 p.m.*
Subject*: Better numbers*

Hi, all,

Joel here. Well, Eliza and I had a good weekend together. More smiles, playing, laughs, and good naps. She has not vomited recently but has had very messy diapers—at least things are moving in the right direction! Her creatinine came down to 5.2 this morning (it was 5.9 at its worst last week), and her phosphorus is now under 10. The doctor was very pleased about the numbers, especially that the phosphorus was no longer in "double digits." He said that if her numbers continue to look better tomorrow, we may not have to put her on hemodialysis. Please continue to pray her "bad" numbers to continue to drop! We still haven't seen any urine for the past few days, but she has been dehydrated from dialysis, vomiting, and diarrhea, so…?

I did get a chance to see Facing the Giants *with my dad-in-law and another friend. Go see it! (And this coming from a guy who never watches football—ever!)*

There's a point in the movie where a man says, "Two farmers were praying for rain. One farmer plowed and planted seed, and the other did not. Which farmer believed that God would send rain?"

So please pray for clarity for Shannon and me to know how to "prepare for rain" in faith. I want to have faith in God and His promises, not *the promises I wish He would make. I want to live in faith, believe that nothing is impossible for God, but also ask His will be done, in His timing, for His glory.*

I really loved the movie and applaud them for its integrity. I wish there were more movies out there like it. However, it is somewhat predictable in that the "man of faith" has a "happily ever after" (as if we really thought the football team would lose). What about the times when God chooses not to give us the ending we want? Although Peter was released miraculously from prison by an angel (Acts 12), James, the brother of John, was put to death with the sword (Acts 12:2). Paul had a thorn in the flesh (2 Cor. 12:7–10) that the Lord did not take away, and Timothy had frequent stomach illness (1 Tim. 5:23) that he had to treat with "medicine" rather than a miraculous cure.

I absolutely believe that the same God Almighty who created the whole universe with a word needs to only speak a word to completely restore Eliza. I know that while He allows suffering, He never causes it. I will still love Him and believe He is loving and strong (Ps. 62:11–12). Please join us in prayer, that we would know how to prepare for rain in faith for His glory!

Thanks so much for hanging in there with us. And thanks be to God, who became a child so that He could also be with *us.*

"The virgin will be with child and will give birth to a son, and they will call Him Immanuel" (Matt. 1:23), which means, "God with us."

—*Joel*

Moving On

Sent: *Monday, October 16, 2006, 6:51 p.m.*
Subject: *One day at a time*

It's Monday, the day we've been waiting for all week-end. The final numbers are in, and praise God, Eliza will not be undergoing hemodialysis today! Her creatinine stayed the same, and her phosphorus numbers were down to a 9.7 (they would like to see this number down to a 6; normal is 0.4–0.9). She has not thrown up in forty-eight hours, and she's playful, even walking around her crib, coloring, playing with Play-Doh, and being a kid—a tethered kid, but a kid. The doctors continue to marvel that her attitude and playfulness don't reflect the state of her lab reports. She's such a sweet girl, offering her teddy bears to the nurses and visitors.

However, Eliza faces a new challenge today: a herniated belly button. Thankfully, Zoë had one at birth, so it doesn't freak me out. But it's not necessarily good news for Eliza. It's evidence that her small frame is having a hard time with the fluid volume from the peritoneal dialysis. As the doctor put it, we're basically making her pregnant with all the fluid, and when she spent most of her time lying down, it didn't bother her, but now that she's active again, it's caused her belly button to pop. This may be a sign that hemodialysis would be a better option for her. I know she really doesn't want Eliza to be on hemo, but if her hernia gets much bigger, she may not have a choice.

They are still keeping Eliza on twenty-four-hour peritoneal dialysis but decreasing the cycles to twelve, meaning fluid would drain and fill every two hours. I'm happy for this change since it was draining and filling every hour. She usually cries at the end of each fill cycle from the abdominal pressure, making it hard to sleep. Pray for my mom, as she is staying with her tonight. I only got a few hours' sleep last night since she cries every hour and nurses come in every two hours to do "something"— check blood pressure, give her medication, start her tube feeding, weigh her, draw blood, etc. It makes for really long nights. I keep wondering how long we can continue at this rate—we could all use more sleep. My dad is getting over a sore throat, which has taken him out of the rotation the last few nights. We can't lose a man now! Pray for his strength, physically as well as emotionally.

So here are our hopes, that, one, Eliza's numbers will continue to go down, allowing them to decrease the fill volume with each cycle. My goodness, they are putting 550 grams into her with each cycle—that's the amount a normal kid pees every day! A decrease in fluid would allow her hernia to improve or prevent it from getting worse. We are also hoping that as Eliza's numbers improve, she'll get more of her freedom back. She is having a hard time being tethered. She often walks as far as she can to the door and then points with a pouty face. It's hard not having the freedom to take her to the playroom, as active as she is. The dialysis nurse gave me a quick word of advice today: since we're still responsible for tearing down and setting up her dialysis machine, she suggested we run her down to the playroom for a half-hour between her twenty-four-hour cycles since we'll have to restart the machine anyway. Great idea! And we're not breaking any "rules" or doctor's orders!

On the home front, Zoë was in dire need of more attention and love, so we've sent her to a friend's house for a few days. I'm struggling with it, feeling like I'm dumping my kid on someone else, but I couldn't stand seeing her watch so much TV and become such a bully to Robin just to get attention. We have all had such limited energy combined with the undercurrent of stress—we're struggling to keep up with her. I know she was sad about the decision to leave, but I'm trusting she's having a good time. Pray for her, that she wouldn't feel forgotten or unloved. I know kids adjust well, but I also know Zoë is a very smart little girl with complex emotions that she doesn't know how to express.

Robin, on the other hand, is having the time of her life as the "only" child—she's a riot! As I was leaving last night for the hospital, she saw me packing Eliza's freshly washed blankie. Sensing I was leaving, she followed me around, saying, "I coming, I coming." She disappeared for a minute and then reappeared at the front door carrying her own blankie. "I coming, I coming!" She misses Eliza. We all do. We are all longing to get back to some normal rhythm.

Choosing to rest and living in today's victories,
Shannon

God brought me to Hebrews 10:35–39 this weekend! May He help me to not shrink back!

Sent: *Wednesday, October 18, 2006, 10:44 a.m.*
Subject: *Yes again!*

Eliza's creatinine is down to 4.3 today, and her phosphorus is down to 6.9—does it get any sweeter than that? The doctor has decided to cut back her dialysis to twenty hours, so she will have a four-hour break this afternoon. We are meeting with a reporter from The Oklahoman *today, and if things stay on schedule, Eliza's story should be in the paper tomorrow. It's funny how things come back around. Joel was in the paper earlier this year (for his prosthetic work), and we are meeting with the same reporter today along with a good friend who is also a reporter. Dear, sweet Lindsay has had to keep her mouth shut over there at* The Oklahoman *headquarters this entire time! I admire her patience and willingness to be there for us and watch out for our family regarding the media.*

I'm off. God bless each of you!

Shannon

Photo taken for The Oklahoman newspaper

Zoe holding the newspaper where our story was on the front page

In Philippians 4:4, we're told to "rejoice in the Lord always. I will say it again: Rejoice!" In the midst of the storm, we have to be reminded to rejoice *always in the Lord*, not in our circumstances. They will always change, but God will not. He is the same yesterday, today, and forever. We can rejoice in who He is, not in what we think He is doing. First Thessalonians 5:16–18 also tells us, "Rejoice always, pray continually, give thanks in all circumstances; for this is God's will for you in Christ Jesus." Hard times definitely help us to pray without ceasing, but are we seriously going to look at rejoicing always and, in everything, giving thanks? God makes it clear this is His will for us, to rejoice, pray, and give thanks in *all* circumstances. What a call! How can we do this?

Romans 8:28 holds a precious key to victory for us found in Jesus. It's a favorite of many but is often misused. "And we know that in all things God works for the good of those who love him, who have been called according to his purpose." Is Eliza's illness really for our good? Illness isn't good, so this *E. coli* must not be according to

171

His purposes, right? What does this verse mean by *good* and *purposes*? If I want a car, do I get it because I think it would be good for me? And surely, I could use it for God's purposes by carpooling others to church, right? It's easy to interpret this verse through our own lens, picking and choosing what we deem as "good" and "God's purposes," but in order to really understand verse 28, we must keep reading verse 29, "To be conformed to the image of his Son, that He might be the firstborn among many brothers and sisters."

God *promises* to work *all* things for the good of those who love Him and are called according to His purpose, which is to be conformed to the image of Jesus! He hasn't promised any particular outcome other than conforming us to the image of His Son, our Savior and brother! But we can rejoice always, knowing that God is working all things for our good eternally, to make us look more like Him. Regardless of the final outcome of any given circumstance, God's purpose is to make us look like Him. Once I get this truth from my head into my heart, then I can start to see that I can rejoice always. No matter what, I'm the winner in the end. We can say a hardy "Amen" with James. "Consider it pure joy, my brothers and sisters, whenever you face trials of many kinds, because you know that the testing of your faith produces perseverance. Let perseverance finish its work so that you may be mature and complete, not lacking anything."

Jesus doesn't want us to lack anything, which is why I can sing, "Yes, Lord, yes, Lord, I am pressured, but not crushed. Persecuted, not abandoned. Struck down, but not destroyed. I am blessed beyond the curse, for His promise will endure, that His joy's going to be my strength."

I have been greatly challenged by Corrie and Betsie Ten Boom's example in their shared story *The Hiding Place*, written about their Holocaust experience during World War II.

> The move to permanent quarters came the second week in October. We were marched, ten abreast, along the wide cinder avenue... Several times the column halted while numbers were read out— names were never used at Ravensbruck. At last Betsie's and mine were called... We stepped out

of line with a dozen or so others and stared at the long gray front of Barracks 28. "Fleas!" I cried. "Betsie, the place is swarming with them!" We scrambled across the intervening platforms, heads low to avoid another bump, dropped down to the aisle and hedged our way to a patch of light. "Here! And here another one!" I wailed. "Betsie, how can we live in such a place!" "Show us. Show us how." It was said so matter-of-factly it took me a second to realize she was praying. More and more the distinction between prayer and the rest of life seemed to be vanishing for Betsie. "Corrie!" she said excitedly. "He's given us the answer! Before we asked, as He always does! In the Bible this morning. Where was it? Read that part again!" I glanced down the long dim aisle to make sure no guard was in sight, then drew the Bible from its pouch. "It was in First Thessalonians," I said. We were on our third complete reading of the New Testament since leaving Scheveningen. In the feeble light I turned the pages. "Here it is: Comfort the frightened, help the weak, be patient with everyone. See that none of you repays evil for evil, but always seek to do good to one another and to all..." It seemed written expressly to Ravensbruck. "Go on," said Betsie. "That wasn't all." "Oh yes:... Rejoice always, pray constantly, give thanks in all circumstances; for this is the will of God in Christ Jesus." "That's it, Corrie! That's His answer. Give thanks in all circumstances! That's what we can do. We can start right now to thank God for every single thing about this new barracks!" I stared at her; then around me at the dark, foul-aired room. "Such as?" I said. "Such as being assigned here together." I bit my lip. "Oh yes, Lord Jesus!" "Such as what you're holding in your hands." I looked down at the Bible. "Yes! Thank You, dear Lord, that there was no inspection when we entered here! Thank You for all these women, here in this room, who will meet You in these pages." "Yes," said Betsie, "Thank You for the very crowding here. Since we're packed so close, that many more will hear!" She looked at me expectantly. "Corrie!" she prodded. "Oh, all right. Thank You for the jammed, crammed, stuffed, packed suffocating crowds." "Thank You," Betsie went on serenely, "for the fleas and for—" The fleas! This was too much. "Betsie, there's no way even God can make me grateful for a flea." "Give thanks in all circumstances," she quoted. "It doesn't say, 'in pleasant circumstances.' Fleas are part of this place where God has put us." And so we stood between tiers of bunks and gave thanks for fleas. But this time I was sure Betsie was wrong.[16]

Corrie later realized the truth in their confession of thanks, as the fleas were the catalyst to keeping the Nazi officers out of their barracks, protecting them from further abuse. God had provided a place of rest and safety in the midst of horror. He had used the fleas for their good, whether they saw it at first or not—they had reason to be thankful! The Lord was working for their good!

There's great warning in Romans 1:20–22, "For since the creation of the world God's invisible qualities—his eternal power and divine nature—have been clearly seen, being understood from what has been made, so that people are without excuse. *For although they knew God* [italics mine], they neither glorified him as God nor gave thanks to him, but their thinking became futile and their foolish hearts were darkened. Although they claimed to be wise, they became fools."

---

[16] Corrie ten Boom, Elizabeth Sherrill, and John Sherrill, *The Hiding Place* (New York: Bantam Books, 1971).

We are all without excuse before the Lord concerning His nature and eternal power. There are those who *know God* but choose to neither glorify nor give Him thanks—in all circumstances. When things don't go their way, they scream and cuss out God, blaming Him for their pain. As we continue to read in Romans 1, this mindset leads to backsliding in the life of a believer. "They exchanged the truth about God for a lie, and worshiped and served created things rather than the Creator—who is forever praised. Amen." This depraved mind can continue to slide into all kinds of evil, as the chapter continues. Where did this start? By choosing to not glorify God or give Him thanks in all things. Which altar are we worshiping at, the Lord's or our own? *Lord, help me to rejoice in Your love and presence always. Help me to be thankful for these "fleas" in my life. They may be annoying and painful today but will serve a purpose in the long run—I will choose to rest in that.*

Sent: *Wednesday, October 18, 2006, 7:30 p.m.*
Subject: *Channel 9 News—tonight!*

We are going to be on Channel 9 News tonight, Wednesday, at 10:00 p.m. Wow! Things sure escalated today regarding the media. Our story has "hit the press" and will be on our local doorsteps tomorrow morning. We'll be on the front page!

Love,
Shannon

*****

Sent: *Friday, October 20, 2006, 11:10 a.m.*
Subject: *Day 39*

Eliza seems to be improving in leaps and bounds each day! I'm still in shock and a bit reserved since every time she does well, she seems to backslide. But yesterday, Thursday, Eliza's creatinine was down to 3.6 (she finally made it below the 4 mark!), and her phosphorus remained the same in the upper-6 range. She was super happy yesterday and loved all the attention she received throughout the day. I never knew that a two-year-old could ham it up so much, but she batted her long lashes at everyone yesterday. As we passed one man in the hall on our way to the playroom (during her four-hour break from dialysis), he said, "Hey, isn't that the girl I saw in the paper this morning?" She just beamed at him—obviously, she knows something is going on that involves her.

On Wednesday, her tube feedings were increased to every 4.5 hours or thereabouts—she's getting five feedings a day. They have also increased the volume of each feeding to almost double the previous amount (she's now ingesting five cans of Ensure a day instead of one to two)! My dad and I think they are trying to get her full nutrition to see how her body will respond to it. Since she's getting everything she needs through her tube, she has not eaten or had anything to drink by mouth in several days, but the doctors are not surprised or concerned. They just want to see what happens to her numbers. And the good news is that she has not thrown up, until this morning, but she was really angry at the nurses during her blood draw, and that may have caused her to toss her cookies. We aren't concerned since it has been three to four days since she threw up from nausea.

This morning, Friday, Eliza's creatinine dropped again to 3.1! Her phosphorus is finally in the normal range at 5.9! Praise Jesus! Her doctor has decided to cut her dialysis back from twenty hours to sixteen hours. The doctor is still unwilling to give us any idea about when we may be discharged—I know they are just as eager to get Eliza home, but we need her numbers to continue stabilizing, and then we need to maintain them for a few days. So perhaps if she continues on this path, it could be next week sometime?

Here's the biggest news of all—as far as I'm concerned, anyhow: the amount of pee Eliza is outputting seems to be slowly increasing. Yesterday she outputted 142 grams of just pee—that's a whole lot more than the 40 grams she began with! Is her output going to continue increasing? I sure hope and pray so! The doctor hasn't made any comment about this yet. We have been told that it is possible to have "bad pee" that doesn't have any creatinine in it—meaning the kidneys are not processing it as they should. So join us in praying that Eliza's output would be "good pee" and that it would continue to increase.

Here is the question of the day: Is Eliza's creatinine level decreasing in such great amounts because she's been on twenty-hour dialysis, or could it be that her kidneys are starting to do more of the work themselves?

Sidenote: Channel 4 ran Eliza's story last night. It is the feature story on Oklahoma Fox today, and we're wondering if we'll hear from Channel 5. Here is what Stacey (the reporter) from Channel 9 e-mailed our friend at The Oklahoman*: "What an absolutely wonderful family. Those three girls are doll babies."*

Eliza's name, Eliza Grace. Eliza means "consecrated: to devote irrevocably to the worship of God." When we put her name together, it means "consecrated to God through grace." It's our prayer that the Lord do exactly that! It is by grace that she has been saved to the glory of God! Thank you so much for walking this road with us—it has meant a great deal to us! Each of you has played a role in the miracle that is unfolding before us!

Love,
Shannon

The Lord appears to accentuate names through the fabric of Scripture. *Abram* was changed to *Abraham* in Genesis 17:5, and *Sarai* to *Sarah* soon after. Jacob's name was changed to Israel in Genesis 32:28, and in John 1:42 we see Jesus change Simon's name to Peter. And my personal favorite from Revelation 2:17 says, "Whoever has ears, let them hear what the Spirit says to the churches. To the one who is victorious, I will give some of the hidden manna. I will also give that person a white stone with a *new name* [italics mine] written on it, known only to the one who receives it." How exciting! For those found in Christ, there is a new name waiting for us, one that only the Father knows and will share only with the recipient. I often wonder with pure glee what that stone will hold for me.

Since scripture indicates that names are important and meaningful to God, we chose to prayerfully consider our girls' names during my pregnancies. We didn't want to choose just anything; we wanted their names to be of the Lord. After we had searched through the thick, ominous name book for weeks, the Lord clearly led Joel to the name Zoë for our eldest. To be honest, I wasn't too keen on it at first. I had been working in downtown Seattle, playing the role of professional, and couldn't imagine how I'd react to be handed a business card with the name Zoë on it—is it sophisticated enough? After all, the only Zoë I knew was an orange animated puppet on a popular children's television show. Tells you where my aspirations were at that time! Thankfully, Joel was persistent, and after learning of its meaning, I agreed. Zoë is the Greek word for *life*, but not just any life; it means *abundant life*! Overflowing, gushing *life*!

With her being my first child, we painfully watched the "grass grow" that last week of my pregnancy, which slowly ebbed into week

41. Day after day we waited with great anticipation for Zoë's arrival, only to be met with sleepless nights, anxious, bored relatives, and swollen ankles. But as is always the case, the Lord had a plan. Exactly one week late, Zoë was born at sunrise on Easter morning! Life! Jesus came, died a hideous death, and rose again at sunrise on Easter to give us life! Not just any life, but overflowing, victorious, gushing life! And there she was, our little Zoë, brimming with new life. Her middle name, Ann, means "blessed by grace," so put them together and her name means "life blessed by grace." Is our Lord good or what? How could we have ever guessed she'd be born on Easter?

Little Robin, our little bird. She was so active in utero that I was sure she'd find a way out one way or another, despite her serene sister relegated to her share of space. My left side was always quiet and peaceful, while my right...well, it was a constant dance. I told Joel one night, "We need to name this one Robin since she's flighty like a bird!" Her middle name, Renae, means "born again." So her name put together is "little bird born again." The significance of her name would become profound to us in the years to come.

Sent: Saturday, October 21, 2006, 12:57 p.m.
Subject: More pee!

Yesterday, Friday, Eliza outputted 206 grams of pee! That's a lot, as far as we're concerned! But is it enough? I mentioned before that Eliza could potentially output "bad pee," and Joel asked this morning whether or not they would ever choose to test the creatinine levels in her pee. The doctor replied that it wouldn't be worth their time; she said they get all the information they need from her blood draws. Are you ready for today's lab report? I can't say it without beaming—her creatinine level is 2.8, and her phosphorus has remained at 6! That is good, given the increase in her nutrition.

The biggest question of the day, Will she get to come home soon? The doctor was still hesitant to answer but said, "Maybe this week," with a great emphasis on maybe. She would like to see Eliza maintain these lower numbers for a few days. She decreased the dialysis again today down to twelve hours with six cycles. She said she's not willing to send Eliza home on more than six cycles. So we hope that her numbers continue to go down or stay the same over the next few days.

Unfortunately, Eliza has been running a low-grade fever since yesterday morning. They are monitoring her closely for potential infections. This could also delay her homecoming. If she should require antibiotics, they would keep her longer (I think antibiotics usually run over ten days?). We can't bring her home with an IV, which she currently has running in a vein on the top of her left foot. It's been conveniently covered by her slippers and hasn't hindered her walking for the past week. She has been receiving IV iron to help bond with the medicine she's getting to help her digest food. She, of course, is still tube feeding. She will definitely be coming home with it, but thankfully, the doctor said most kids show more interest in food once home. In the meantime, we would need to contact the nephrologists' unit once a week to inform them of her food intake. They would then make decisions based on what we report. So she could be tube-feeding for several more weeks? Good thing we've been bringing home all the extra Ensure cans she has had stacked up in her room. Our insurance won't cover it, and I know they're expensive. Hopefully, we've stocked up enough.

I was totally shocked and humbled yesterday when my mom received a call while caring for Eliza from a sincere thirty-two-year-old man who has offered to donate one of his kidneys to Eliza!

Who does that? I'm amazed and feel like I just saw an example of Jesus with skin on. A total stranger who is willing to give a part of himself for Eliza's restoration, not because of anything we've done, but because he has died to himself and loves Jesus. Amazing! May I be more like him.

In John 10:9–11, Jesus said, "I am the gate; whoever enters through me will be saved. He will come in and out, and find pasture. The thief comes only to steal, kill and destroy; I have come that they may have life, and have it to the full. 'I am the good shepherd. The good shepherd lays down his life for the sheep.'"

Love,
Shannon

Homecoming

Sent: *Monday, October 23, 2006, 4:24 p.m.*
Subject: *Is it time?*

Wow! There seems to be a lot of buzz around Eliza's hospital room, preparing for her to come home! Ahhh! I'm elated and terrified at the same time! Where is the dialysis machine going to go? Where are Robin and Eliza going to sleep? What about Zoë? Will her room get overtaken as well? Do we have all the equipment needed? Have we contacted the electric company to have us on a priority list should there be a power outage? Etc., etc., etc.

Yesterday, Sunday, Eliza's creatinine lowered again to 2.7, but her phosphorus went back up to 7. The increased phosphorus was not a surprise since they had to cut her calcium carbonate medicine to see if her body could handle the phosphorus on her own. The calcium carbonate binds with the phosphorus in her food, helping control her phosphorus levels. So this just means she isn't ready to cut that medicine yet.

She outputted 370 grams of pee that we know of! Yeah! Last night they changed her dialysis solution from 1.5 percent strength back up to 2.5 percent since her blood pressure was high, and the night before, Saturday, the dialysis only pulled 162cc of fluid from her system; that number has been in the 500–600cc range in the past. Since she had more retained fluid than necessary, they changed the solution to pull off the remainder. They were also hoping to lower her phosphorus. Here is the key: to make sure that her dialysis output combined with her pee output total the nine hundred grams of Nepro shake she's getting each day. What goes in must come out, one way or another. Oh, her fever is gone! We think she may have had the same cold virus we've been cycling through the house since she's been sneezing.

Eliza's blood work this morning, Monday, showed that her creatinine level remained the same at 2.7, but her phosphorus went up again to 8—too high! They are putting her back on the 1.5 percent strength solution but increasing her cycles from six to seven, which means fourteen hours of dialysis a day. The doctor is hoping that the extra cycle will help lower her phosphorus too.

Joel asked about the increase in Eliza's pee, and the doctor answered with this: Eliza is outputting one milliliter of pee per one kiloliter of her own body weight per hour. The norm is two milliliters of pee for every kiloliter of body weight. However, she said that some would argue that one milliliter is enough. Hmm? Makes me wonder. The question of the day shall remain: Is Eliza making enough of her own pee? The doctors are certainly not ready to take her off dialysis anytime soon, so we'll just keep trekking, trusting their expertise. But we are still hopeful that someday soon, Eliza will be able to sustain life without dialysis! Lord, You are able!

So now on to the good news. Drumroll, please. If—and I stress if—Eliza's phosphorus levels go down tomorrow morning, they may be sending her home! If her levels don't go down, we will just ride it out until they do, which may be a few days. However, doctors and administrators are all hope-

ful that Eliza will make it home this week. Praise God! I hardly know what to do with myself, and yet there's a ton to do to prepare for my baby to come home! Our resident doctor called Joel today to ask him, "Are you guys ready? I mean, are you really ready for her to be home?" Tough question. Yes and no! We want her home, but it's going to be a lot of work. Pray for energy!

Until tomorrow,
Shannon

*****

Sent: *Tuesday, October 24, 2006, 9:32 a.m.*
Subject: *Yeah!*

I just got the call this morning—Eliza is officially being discharged from the hospital today! Yeah! I'm on my way to the hospital to collect all our stuff, including our darling girl. I had a long, frustrating phone conversation this morning with our local nursing company that will supply her tube feeding machine and whatnot. I guess our insurance company is refusing to cover her home feedings! They were going to but have now decided it's not deemed medically necessary. Huh? Please pray that it would all work out. It's very expensive without any coverage. Thanks!

Today is the day!

Skipping,
Shannon

As I walked through the familiar doors at Children's Hospital that morning, tears of joy and loss flowed freely. So much had happened in these halls the past forty-two days, causing me to lose a sense of parental innocence, becoming too familiar with the pain of childhood suffering and loss. The world outside these concrete walls protected me from the realities of such things, but walking these familiar corridors, I reflected on all the children we saw come and go during our days among them. They were no longer strangers but fellow sojourners, parents seeking the best for their loved ones through tears, twenty-four-hour bedside vigils, and hope. Joy bubbled as I pictured carrying Eliza to our car and leaving it all behind. She had been given her golden ticket to freedom, and I couldn't wait to carry her past the threshold! Did she have any concept of what this day meant for her? Home—such a sweet word with profound meaning.

Entering her room, I was taken aback by its bareness. My dad had already packed most of our belongings, and the room had been stripped of everything familiar but happy faces. A joyful nurse entered carrying a box of supplies. "Oh, Shannon, I'm so glad to see you! Today's the day! Before you leave, we have to be sure you're prepared for tube feedings and shots. I'm going to have to witness you inserting a tube in Eliza's nose and administering shots in her thigh before she can be discharged." Really? *All right, Lord, if this is what it takes to get her home, then let me do this efficiently! You know how I feel about needles.*

Holding Eliza down on the bed, I successfully pushed the nose tube up her left nostril until she chose, crying and gagging, to swallow it. *Done. Help me do this, Lord. I'm supposed to be her comforter, not the one inflicting pain, and yet I know this is for her good.* "Good job, Shannon. Now take the stethoscope and listen to her lungs to be sure you don't hear gurgling sounds. We want to be sure the tube is going to her stomach, not her lungs." Accomplishing the task, I handed the instrument back to her. "Oh, no, that's for you. You're going to need it at home." *Oh, goody, I just earned myself a stethoscope!* "Now let's lay her on the bed, allowing her legs to hang over the edge. Go ahead and press your body against her lower legs, swab her thigh with the alcohol pad, and quickly pinch her leg as you insert the needle. The faster you act, the less it will hurt." Through unshed tears, I followed each step, finishing the job with decorated Band-Aids. As

I scooped Eliza in my arms, we both cried. "I'm sorry, baby. We'll have to get through this together, all right? They're just shots, honey. I know you've endured much more than that!"

Handing me a complete sheet of fifteen prescriptions, the nurse instructed I take Eliza on a walk to the main building, a block away, to pick them up at the hospital pharmacy so we could discuss them before discharge. Strapping Eliza into her umbrella stroller, I welcomed the walk and chance to escape with her. Walking past the playroom, I grinned, knowing this was the farthest I had ventured with her since she had been admitted. I pushed through the front doors, and a gush of fall air flooded our senses, causing Eliza to giggle. "Feels good, doesn't it? Just imagine, playing outside again in the backyard!"

After waiting an hour for the pharmacy to complete our order, I quickly walked back, longing to get home. Turning the bend near the nurse's station toward Eliza's room, I noticed crepe paper dangling like curtains over the entryway. "Eliza, what do you think that is?" Grabbing for the strips, I pushed her into the room to the sound of great cheers and laughter. "Eliza's going home! Yeah, Eliza!" A large majority of the nursing staff had gathered in her room, wearing crepe paper hairdos and happy smiles, one choosing to come in on her day off! They took turns fawning over us, blowing bubbles with Eliza, and loving us through hugs. Tears were shared with many happy stories of Eliza's gentle heart and patience with the staff. My heart radiated feeling the love and joy from these women who had longed for her return home just as we had. Thanks flowed as we remembered their tenderness toward Eliza—gently cleaning her hair after throwing up, keeping her bundled when cold, offering toys when sought. Countless hours of compassion and care for all of us.

In the midst of the revelry, Channel 9 News appeared in the hallway, longing to capture her homecoming. We spent time talking with them as they filmed us preparing to leave. Strapping Eliza into her car seat in my dad's car after six weeks felt strange as she scowled at me, unsure of the commotion. "It's okay, baby, we're going home. You get to come with us today. Look, wave bye-bye to the hospital!"

As we pulled into our driveway, Eliza's eyes began to brighten. No sooner had my dad had her out of her car seat than Robin came bounding out of the house. She stopped, giggling at Eliza, arms swinging in excitement. Eliza wobbled into a good standing position before she slowly began taking steps toward her, extending her arms, her nose tube and dialysis tube pinned to the back of her shirt the only reminders she had just left the hospital. Robin finally bounded to her full force, hugging her. What a sweet reunion for these twins, all captured by Channel 9 news for us to enjoy for years to come!

We settled into the family room, and the news anchor began asking me questions about our journey. At that time, I naively thought having Eliza home would be easier, but the weeks to come would challenge everything I had come to know about myself and my faith. In some ways, our journey was just beginning.

> **Sent**: *Tuesday, October 24, 2006, 5:33 p.m.*
> **Subject**: *Channel 9 news, again, tonight!*
>
> *Eliza's homecoming is going to be aired tonight, Tuesday, at ten o'clock, on Channel 9 News!* The Oklahoman *is coming tomorrow morning for another interview.*
>
> *Today's thought: God's faithfulness, Zofran.*
>
> *As Joel and I were walking into church on Sunday, I reached my hand into my coat pocket. As I was warming my hands, I felt an unfamiliar object. Curious, I pulled it out to find a small crinkled package that brought back a flood of memories. I turned it over and saw the word* Zofran *spelled in large print. I smiled at myself as I had purposely left this small package in my coat pocket two years ago to remind me of God's faithfulness.*
>
> *When I was pregnant with the twins, I was put on a medication called Zofran to help me with nausea during the first trimester. I was losing too much weight, especially in light of carrying twins, which*

prompted my doctor to prescribe the medication. It's typically prescribed to patients on chemotherapy, as it's known for its ability to decrease nausea. I kept the small crinkled package to remind me of just how faithful God was to us during my pregnancy. I carried those girls to thirty-nine weeks and finally had to be induced since they had no inclination of coming on their own. We had a good, textbook delivery—twice! They weighed thirteen pounds between them. Very healthy babies. God was so good.

I have found myself strangely connected to Eliza through Zofran, as it has been prescribed to her as well. Every time the nurses administer it to her, I think to myself, Oh, that's the good stuff. You want that! Trust me, you'll be feeling great within minutes! *It's become a symbol of God's faithfulness to me. I think I'll add one of the labels from her syringes to my coat pocket so that in a few years from now, I can be reminded once again of how God has carried us through a challenging time.*

Love,
Shannon

Home

Sent: *Thursday, October 26, 2006, 3:53 p.m.*
Subject: *Scheduled chaos*

After forty-two days in the hospital, nine doctors, two resident doctors, a dietician, two case managers, a social worker, close to fifty nurses, ten IVs, somewhere near sixty blood draws, surgery, peritoneal dialysis, a blood transfusion, four chest x-rays, an ultrasound, an MRI, around eight nose feeding tubes, fifteen medications (that I know of), one season change, two renewed hospital parking passes, and countless hours of Animal Planet, Eliza is finally settling back home.

I never pictured myself a nurse, but I have just received a crash course and I have great respect for all in the nursing profession! Since Eliza has returned home, we have been running around like chickens with our heads cut off. It may be a while before we fall into a regular routine, but until then, we've had what I like to call scheduled chaos. Our mornings and evenings are pure craziness. Eliza is still tube feeding five times a day, which is fine, but she's tethered to the feeding machine attached to an IV pole, causing complications. I have found myself running around after her, dragging the pole with us. If I get out of her sight line, she accidentally disconnects herself, trying to find me, spilling sticky formula all over the place. My dad has been feed-

191

ing Eliza around 11:00 p.m. to 12:00 a.m., and Joel has been getting up for her 6:00 a.m. feeding. We are hoping to adjust her feedings to four times a day, hopefully cutting back on the late-night/early-morning feeding. We just need her to be able to handle larger amounts of food in one feeding without throwing it up. I think she may be ready for it, but if not, I have our handy Zofran ready.

Eliza is currently taking five medications a day, twice a day (we were sent home with fifteen medications for dialysis, high blood pressure, etc.), so we're trying to coordinate those with her feedings as much as possible. It's a lot of charting and keeping track of what she took and when. I gave her shot today without any problems, with my dad holding her down. I'm not sure what that will look like once I'm alone; that may have to be an evening activity with Joel.

Robin is thrilled *to have her sister back. As my mom was changing her this morning, she pointed to Eliza's crib and said with a grin, "Liza back." They are adjusting to each other slowly. The first evening was all fun and games, but yesterday the stakes got much higher. The jealously and competition for Mommy, toys, and books was out of control. They did a lot of bantering back and forth, rolling on the floor in frustration, and crying to Mommy (yes, they're two!). Today is getting better. I think they are readjusting to each other and learning how to share again. They had a fun time playing "stroller derby" this morning. They were racing each other with their play baby strollers. Robin chose to be flashy by racing her red Elmo doll, while Eliza chose to be more conservative with her traditional baby doll. It was really fun watching them giggle and race each other around the island in the kitchen.*

Eliza was sent home on fourteen hours of dialysis, which is hard all around. The machine is stuck in her room, which means we either have to play in her room two hours before bed (which is generally dinnertime) or stay in her room two hours after she's woken up (breakfast time). Once my parents leave, it will be hard to coordinate feeding the girls and leaving Eliza in her room. Alone? How is that going to pan out? It would be so much easier if they would cut her hours back to twelve, but in the meantime, we need lots of patience. They don't make longer tubes on this particular set of dialysis tubing since it's so small, which means Eliza only has a five-foot radius. Pray that they would cut her hours soon!

We were told that we no longer need to weigh Eliza's diapers, but that has been the best part of our craziness. Yesterday, Eliza had a 200-gram diaper! It was actually heavier than Robin's! We were so excited that we just had to take a picture of it! It does appear that her pee output is slowly increasing, as yesterday she had a total of 385 grams (I believe 550 grams would be normal for her)! Praise God!

*****

Sent: *Saturday, October 28, 2006, 12:32 p.m.*
Subject: *Lab report*

We have the results back from Eliza's blood draw from Thursday morning. You ready? She's getting better, slowly but surely! Her creatinine was down to 2.4, and her phosphorous was an astonishing 4.2! Remember the doctor was hoping to keep her creatinine around 4, which is good for patients on peritoneal dialysis (normal is 0.4–0.9), so the fact that she keeps going down is really, really good! The doctor was also hoping to keep her phosphorus around 6 (normal is 3.8–6.5), so her body is finally starting to regulate it more! Praise God! She's slowly improving. When she was discharged from the hospital on Tuesday, her phosphorus was 7.1, so that number has greatly improved in just a few days!

The only bummer is Eliza's BUN number. BUN (blood urea nitrogen) is a test that measures her amount of urea nitrogen (a breakdown product of protein metabolism) in the blood. The BUN test is a somewhat-routine test used primarily to evaluate renal (kidney) function. Normal is 7–18, and Eliza is all the way up to 59! Yikes! We would really like to see this number go down; it's the only one that has remained high over the past several weeks. I certainly hope that this number alone isn't an indication of how well her kidneys are functioning on their own. Everything else seems to be going down. Why not this one? I'm not sure if it's something to be concerned about or not.

Eliza beat her 200-gram diaper today with 220 grams! We are thrilled to see her urine output increasing. We were hoping that she could cut back to twelve hours of dialysis soon, but according to my phone conversation yesterday with her nephrologist, she's not ready to do that. She laughed and said, "Oh, one thing at a time. We want to go forward, not backward." Bummer. So we'll just have to keep waiting and work around it. Eliza's blood pressure was really low again yesterday, down to 65/40, which has prompted the doctor to cut her back to just one blood pressure medicine! Yeah! We brought home three blood pressure medicines, so the fact that she's cut off two of those is exciting. We are praying that her body will be able to maintain the lower blood pressure on its own.

We did have two major victories with the insurance company. They have agreed to pay for both the home feedings and blood pressure medicines. It only took five to six people hammering them (case managers, doctors, benefits coordinator, home nursing care, etc.) to finally agree. Yeah! It's funny how you have insurance in case something like this should happen, then it does happen, and the insurance company isn't willing to pay for the care without major battles.

Eliza ate two bites of banana today. That is the first food we've seen her take by mouth in at least two weeks. She still has no interest in food! The doctors told us that it's common for people with her condition to have limited interest in food at the beginning. I guess her interest is supposed to just "click back on" at some point. Pray that it would be sooner than later! The insurance company has agreed to only cover one month of home feedings.

Yesterday, when my dad and I were changing Eliza's smelly diaper, we both are convinced we heard Robin say, "Holy jammas!" We both looked at each other and started cracking up. Where did she get that from? Did she intend to say it, or was she just jabbering? Whatever the case, it was a riot.

I'm sad to say that Zoë has missed all the homecoming excitement. She is down in Dallas at her cousin's house, hopefully having the time of her life. We had made arrangements for her to go down south during this transition time. There is plenty of fighting and readjusting between the twins to stress me out, so a third party would probably push me over the edge. Zoë will be coming home next week, when, hopefully, I will have more of a routine established and can spend focused time with her.

Please join us in praying that the Lord would continue to provide for this whole mess.

Still walking,
Shannon

*****

Sent: *Tuesday, October 31, 2006, 10:13 p.m.*
Subject: *Flying solo*

My parents officially left yesterday morning, after a fond farewell of putting a feeding tube back in Eliza's nose. She woke up yesterday morning in a puddle of Nepro shake and medicines, which means we basically fed her bed. She must have pulled the tube out before her morning feeding. Crazy girl. It took both my parents holding her down to get the tube back in, and even then it came out of her mouth twice before I hit the jackpot. We had a busy morning meeting with our home-care nurse and Sooner Start, which is a state-run program for kids with disabilities. They asked me a bunch of questions regarding Eliza's mental and physical abilities. Based on their scoring, Eliza has qualified for physical therapy, speech therapy, potentially occupational therapy, and a nutritionist through the state until she's three years old. The specialists will even come to our house for appointments. I don't think it gets much better than that!

Eliza did throw up some yesterday, which we hadn't seen for a while. I'm assuming it happened since she "technically" didn't get her morning medications. She seems fine again today, but it made for a long afternoon.

Eliza's lab results from yesterday's blood draw are in: creatinine down to 2.2, phosphorus up to 5.9, and her BUN has gone up to 61. I called her nephrologist this afternoon to ask about the BUN. Should we be concerned that it's going up? She said she's not concerned since her creatinine is going down. She thinks the BUN may be high due to the amount of protein in the Nepro shake. Still no thoughts of decreasing the dialysis to twelve hours. Bummer. We'll keep waiting. We were given permission to change Eliza's feeding schedule just as long as she gets the same amount of food each day and as long as she can keep the food down. So we are hoping to eventually eliminate the midnight feeding. That would be great—at least Joel thinks that would be great, since he's the one who has been getting up for them since Dad left.

We miss you, Dad!

*****

Sent: *Thursday, November 2, 2006, 9:59 a.m.*
Subject: *Blue clamps*

Yesterday, I discovered firsthand what the box of blue clamps sent home with Eliza's dialysis equipment are used for. After lunch, I was picking Eliza up when I heard a "snap," a squeal from Eliza, and felt liquid draining from her catheter tube. Oh no! As I was holding her in my arms, I looked down and saw her catheter sitting in her high chair and immediately realized what had happened: as I was pulling her out of the high chair, her catheter tube got caught and separated into two parts. This is the tube that connects her to the dialysis machine!

I clamped the tube coming from her abdomen as tightly as I could and ran to her room to find one of those blue clamps the nurses had told me about. After I clamped her off in order to prevent all the fluid in her peritoneal cavity from leaking out, I called the nurses in the dialysis unit at Children's Hospital. They told me to bring her in right away. Oh, man, here we go.

We spent the next two hours in the dialysis unit (which just so happens to be across the hall from ICU, where we began this journey) getting a new catheter and further training on injecting antibiotics into her dialysis solution. It's a clever system, really. The catheter is the end part of Eliza's tubing that connects her to the dialysis machine. She has a tube that is coming out of her abdomen. Halfway between these two tubes is a safety latch, so when it gets too much resistance, it will snap apart, preventing the tubing from getting pulled out of her belly. The more it snaps apart, the shorter her tube becomes, since they have to snip off the end for culturing to test for any infection. Now I know why her tube is so long—it hangs down past her kneecap. The more it snaps off, the greater the risk of infection. So the nurses have asked me to put antibiotics in her solution for the next two nights. That in itself is quite a process. I get the pleasure of mixing my own antibiotics with sterile solution and powder, then injecting it with a syringe into her bag. I'm learning all kinds of new tricks!

Zoë has returned home! She came bounding into the house, talking a mile a minute, yesterday. She was very excited to see her sisters, especially Eliza. She just looked at her in awe—this was the first time she'd seen her since her return home from the hospital. Zoë had so much to share and so many things to show us. I can't get over how much she's appeared to age in the past two months! She's no longer a baby or toddler; she's a little girl with all kinds of ideas and expressions. A twinge of pain ached my heart at the loss of time with her. She helped me get Eliza's medicines ready and showed great interest in helping Eliza tube-feed. I'm realizing that the more I involve her, the better. She wants so badly to help and feel involved. She shared how hard it was to see Eliza in the hospital with all the tubes and machines. I have a feeling this may leave a mark in her heart, as she's old enough to remember.

Eliza woke up vomiting yesterday, which means she may not be ready to increase her feedings. So we'll give her a few more days before we try again. However, I had a sweet moment yesterday with her home-care nurse. It turns out she moonlights in the ER at Children's. She was working the night Eliza was rushed over from All Saints. She told me her account of the events from that crazy night. She said that she received the phone call that gave Eliza's room assignment in ICU just as we were arriving in the ER. That was why the doctor came in and swooped her up and carried her upstairs to the ICU himself. The ER was slammed that night—it was just like the movies. I've always wondered if it ever got that crazy, but now I know firsthand. She also said that Eliza is doing phenomenal, given her condition. She said, "You look at her paperwork and expect to see a sick kid who is in bed, sleeping. Instead you see this highly active kid who looks perfectly normal on the outside." Praise God for this! I know that this is the hand of God working in Eliza. Each of you who have prayed for her have had a hand in this! We can't thank you enough! She's all smiles and giggles! She didn't show one ounce of fear toward the hospital yesterday. She acted as if it were her playground.

As for my heart, I have been wondering what the Lord would have me do with continuous heartache. It hurts so bad—everything seems to hurt so much. I think I'm just now getting around to feeling the pain from almost losing my child, from seeing others lose their children, and from seeing so many sick, hurting children. How should one respond? What do we do with all this? In God fashion, He had a word for me yesterday. I'd like to share it with you, as I know we've all had moments in our lives when we hurt so bad we didn't think we could breathe.

God spoke to me through Oswald Chambers in My Utmost for His Highest, *November 1:*

> *You are not your own. Do you not know that you are not your own? (1 Cor. 6:19). There is no such thing as a private life, or a place to hide in this world, for a man or woman who is intimately aware of and shares in the suffering of Jesus Christ. God divides the private life of His saints and makes it a highway for the world on one hand and for Himself on the other. No human being can stand that unless he is identified with Jesus Christ. We are not sanctified for ourselves. We are called into intimacy with the gospel, and things happen that appear to have nothing to do with us. But God is getting us into fellowship with Himself. Let Him have His way. If you refuse, you will be of no value to God in His redemptive work in*

the world, but will be a hinderance and a stumbling block.

The first thing God does is get us grounded on strong reality and truth. He does this until our cares for ourselves individually have been brought into submission to His way for the purpose of His redemption. Why shouldn't we experience heartbreak? Through those doorways God is opening us ways of fellowship with His Son. Most of us collapse at the first grip of pain (AMEN! Me included!). We sit down at the door of God's purpose and enter a slow death through self-pity. And all the so-called Christian sympathy of others helps us to our deathbed. But God will not. He comes with the grip of the pierced hand of His Son, as if to say, enter into fellowship with Me; arise and shine. If God can accomplish His purposes in this world through a broken heart, then why not thank Him for breaking yours??[17]

Wow! I think I will thank Him. How about you? Will you join me?

*****

---

[17] Oswald Chambers, "You Are Not Your Own," in *My Utmost for His Highest,* ed. James Reimann (Crewe, United Kingdom: Oswald Chambers Publications Assn., Ltd., 1992). Used with permission by Our Daily Bread Publishing, Grand Rapids MI 49501.

Sent: *Monday, November 6, 2006, 9:33 p.m.*
Subject: *Two-week checkup*

Eliza and I ventured back to Children's Hospital today for her two-week follow-up appointment. Things are looking good! Her creatinine is down to 1.9 (normal is 0.4–0.7), and her phosphorus is perfectly normal at 4.4. Praise Jesus! She's doing well enough that they have decreased her dialysis to twelve hours. Ah, I can't tell you what a relief this is! No more trying to juggle three children between the kitchen and the twins' bedroom. Yes! I feel such freedom right now! And to top this off, no more shots for two weeks! Eliza's hemoglobin is doing so well that we've been asked to "please refrain" from her Procrit shots for two weeks. Awe, shucks, do we have to? After two weeks, she will go down to half-strength twice a week. Joel just got out of learning how to give these shots, as tonight was going to be his first! Lucky dog. I guess that's good, since it's his birthday! What a beautiful present!

Eliza has been throwing up in the mornings, five times this past week. She seems to have a hard time keeping the Ensure down after she completes dialysis. In speaking with the doctor about this, he said it doesn't surprise him. "Dialysis does strange things to your body. It's hard to keep food down, and everything tastes bad." It occurred to me that the only time she has shown true interest in food was when she was down to nine hours of dialysis per day in the hospital. Perhaps with the decrease in dialysis, we'll see her able to keep her food down and see her desire increase. Sadly, he said if Eliza should need long-term dialysis or a transplant, we would have to put a feeding tube in her abdomen rather than through her nose, as she would have limited desire for food for a long time. The tube would also be essential for the antirejection medications that are required after a transplant. He said we would wait until next month to decide whether or not to insert the tube. I think it's another surgery. Outpatient, perhaps?

Overall, Eliza is doing really well. She's extremely active! She throws up and then is up and running around before I have time to get her cleaned up. I have a few things to learn from her, like the ability to not complain when I'm uncomfortable. She amazes me.

We received a call from the secretary in the dialysis unit last Friday. She called to tell me that a local GI doctor who had read about Eliza in the newspaper wanted to give us a case of Nepro that a drug rep had left for her. She had no need for it and called our doctor to ask if it would be appropriate for Eliza. We're touched that she went out of her way on our behalf! God is providing! He's awesome!

A few of my thoughts from today:

When Joel and I lived in Seattle, we visited a wildlife reserve on one of the islands. They had wild lions kept behind precarious chain-link fences. As we stopped in front of one of their enclosures, the tour guide said with an authoritative voice, "Lions tend to stalk their prey before they attack. They pick out the weakest and easiest target." As she was saying this, the large, hungry lion paced back and forth behind his fence, panting, full of fire, eyeing us as a child would candy in a candy store. His glance first fell on a toddler riding on his father's shoulders, then he quickly turned to a young boy in a wheelchair, but then he locked his telling eyes on me. He was clearly sizing me up, calculating how fast I could run, what my weaknesses might be, and how easily I'd be captured. It was a terrifying experience for me. Until you've locked eyes with a wild animal, realizing you'd be dead in a matter of minutes, it's hard to understand. I felt his intense stare piercing my very being, even as we had wandered several yards away. He knew exactly where I was in the midst of the crowd around me, which made me long for our car.

I have always pictured God as a lion in my mind, and that experience made it all the more real to me. A few years ago, after the lion incident, I thought of an image of a lion stalking me, running me down and tearing me to shreds. It hurt immensely, but when he was finished, I came forth as gold, shining and brilliant. It was my Savior refining me, shredding all that was not of Him in order to make me beautiful. A few years later, I had another image of myself trying to scratch at my own flesh in hopes of making myself more beautiful or acceptable to my Savior, but what I discovered was that all I had done was create scars that took time to heal. I learned that only God can refine me; only He can search me out, run me down, shred off all that is not of Him, and make me shine. It hurts, oh, does it hurt, but the end result is always incredible, far better than anything I could ever do on my own.

As Lucy asked the Otter in The Chronicles of Narnia, *of Aslan the great lion, "Is he safe?"*

"Of course he's not safe, but he's good."

I second that again and again. I have often asked myself lately, "Since I serve such an incredible God, how could I ever expect to live an ordinary life?" It is my prayer I would forever carry the mark of the lion.

*****

Sent: Wednesday, November 8, 2006, 8:26 p.m.
Subject: Calgon, take me away

I'm trying to keep my cool, but things are really hard right now. Eliza will not stop throwing up! It appears that she's unable to handle any table food right now. It doesn't matter what it is—Nepro shake, Cheerios, animal crackers, or fruit. She just ends up throwing it up. She threw up her nose tube this morning. I think partly because the solid food in her stomach helped kick it up. Joel was unable to come home for lunch, so we went to his work to stuff the feeding tube back up her nose and down her throat, with the help of one of his coworkers. It is truly a three-man job. Robin also woke up with throw-up all over her bed yesterday morning and still won't eat anything. She has a low-grade fever, diarrhea, and just wants to be held. I went through three loads of laundry and two showers with the girls today, just trying to keep things clean. That is, until our washer stopped working. Just stopped running, kaput. So no more laundry capability. Lord, have mercy!

Zoë's also bidding for my attention, and I'm having a hard time being patient. Pray for my strength. I just want to curl up and cry. Can I send myself into time-out?

*****

Sent: Thursday, November 9, 2006, 10:22 a.m.
Subject: Miserable

Thank you so much for all your sentiments this morning. It's so good to know we are covered in prayer right now. I'm sad to say that last night was

205

misery for Joel and me. We were both up till 4:00 a.m., throwing up, holding our stomachs in pain, crying out for mercy. I think it's safe to say our family has been hit with some sort of stomach virus. Zoë threw up this morning as well, but she seems to be doing better now. Eliza is still out cold in her crib, and I'm encouraged that there's no sign of throw-up anywhere. Has she really been spared this? Please, Jesus. Robin is tired and weak, but she has not thrown up yet this morning. Joel is home from work, very weak. We both hurt all over and feel like our bodies have been hit by Mack trucks. I can't remember the last time we were hit this hard by a virus. Talk about literally walking out, "in sickness and in health." We held each other's hands a lot last night! But we praise Jesus that this didn't happen two months ago while we had Eliza in the hospital. The E. coli we had could have been much crueler to our bodies. God was merciful then, and I know He'll be merciful now. Pray for our strength, that we would work well together today to take care of these kids, despite our own pain.

Nothing like Pedialyte popsicles for breakfast!

*****

Sent: *Friday, November 10, 2006, 8:28 a.m.*
Subject: *Ah…*

I'm feeling so much better this morning!! I feel like a whole new woman! I got a good night's sleep on the leather couch with the fan on since I was sweating pretty profusely (probably getting rid of the bug), while Joel was bundled up in our bed, freezing. Thank you so much for praying for us! Joel just left for work, and I'm getting ready for a new day with the girls. Joel is still feeling a bit weak but really needs to go to work; he's very far behind on his paperwork, and some of his patients are here from out of state (he sees and fits prosthetic patients). Plus, he's taking a week off starting next Wednesday while Zoë and I travel to Florida. (We had a family vacation planned that Joel refused to allow me and Zoë to cancel. He's sending us on alone to spend time with my parents while he stays home with the twins. We were able to get a refund from our airline for his flight, thanks to letters from Eliza's doctors.) Zoë told me that her tummy still hurts this morning, so I have her drinking more 7Up. I haven't checked on Eliza and Robin yet.

Tonight, shopping for a new clothes washer! Oh, Eliza has learned a new trick—how to push her own IV pole around the house with her feeding bag attached to it. I love it! She can get anywhere she wants to go now without assistance. One more freedom for me!

Sent: *Friday, November 24, 2006, 1:35 p.m.*
Subject: *Home...*

Zoë and I have returned safely home after a fun week of adventure in Florida. It began with a fairly scary airplane ride from Dallas to Orlando. A combination you don't want to see midair after an hour's delay due to "technical problems"—a rancid smell of burning rubber, smoke in the cabin, really bad turbulence, and flight attendants running down the aisle with a fire extinguisher, asking everyone on the left side of the plane seated over the wing to lift their window shades. I still don't get that. What good was that going to do? Who was going to "open"

*their window for them to put out a fire on the wing
with a small fire extinguisher?*

*After about five minutes of truly feeling like
we were going down and that something had gone
terribly wrong, the pilot finally announced on the
loudspeaker that they had released a "cooling gel"
on the left engine since it had overworked from the
amount of turbulence, but things looked okay for
the remainder of the flight. It was a very long hour
with continued turbulence (the worst I've ever experienced), combined with the rancid smell that never
diminished. There was a cancer survivor in the aisle
next to us. She was wearing a "doctor mask," as Zoë
calls it, to protect herself from further illness. She
was grabbing her table tray with her entire being,
rocking and moaning in fear. I could relate with her
all too well—we didn't come this far just to die in
a plane crash, did we, Lord? I was trying to protect
Zoë from being fearful as much as I could, all the
while battling my own silent shock. But thankfully,
we landed without further complications, just very
queasy stomachs. It took a lot of courage to board
our return flight Wednesday. I keep wondering, Is
the enemy trying to kill us? What is up with all this?*

*However, Zoë and I had a great time at Disney
World. Zoë met more characters than I can recall,
and her favorite ride was the Teacups. We had a
great time reconnecting and laughing together—
such needed focus time as my parents spoiled us.
I felt free for the first time in several months and
enjoyed the distraction Disney provided.*

*Joel, on the other hand…well, let's just say he
really had no idea what he had signed up for. How
could one ever prepare him? It was a very long week
for him, and I came back one of the most appre-
ciated moms ever. But I am truly impressed with*

how clean the house was when we returned and how much he accomplished despite the struggles. He's a super dad and my hero!

As for Eliza, the drama continues. How long, O Lord, how long? Eliza is still throwing up consistently, about five to six times a week. After speaking with my dad about it and doing some research online, we decided it would be wise to call Eliza's nutritionist at Children's. It wasn't long into our conversation that she showed real concern. "It's not normal for her to still be throwing up this much. I'm really concerned for her and think she needs to see a GI specialist." She also voiced concern for Eliza choking on her nose tube while throwing up. "My greatest concern is her safety. She could choke herself." Great, what do we do with that?

Wednesday morning, Joel got a call from the dialysis unit informing him that the earliest any GI doctor at Children's could see Eliza was in two months, so they went ahead and made an appointment for her on December 5 at All Saints Hospital instead. That means we have two big appointments on December 5. We will be taking Eliza that morning to see the nephrologist at Children's, in what I believe could be a very big appointment. I was given the impression they would determine at that time whether or not Eliza needs to be put on a transplant list or whether or not she's doing well enough to cut back on her dialysis. Then we will go from there over to All Saints to see another set of doctors. Why do I feel like we're about to open a whole new can of worms? Eliza has been anything but textbook through this whole process. In two days our month of coverage for her feeding tube expires and we will have to continue fighting for it. We were really hoping she would be eating by now. She has shown a little interest in food, but we are very hesitant to give it to her since it just comes back up.

Based on the research my dad and I did, we're wondering if she has hypercalcemia, which is causing her to have some form of acid reflux. We're amateurs, so we really don't know if that could be the problem, but we do know that her calcium was really, really high at her last appointment. We've been giving her calcium carbonate with each feeding to bind with the phosphorus in her system to try to keep that number down. But now that her phosphorus has remained normal and she's peeing more, perhaps we're still giving her too much calcium? The nephrologist at her last appointment did cut back on the amount of calcium carbonate we're giving her, but maybe it wasn't enough. So the only thing we feel we can do to be proactive is to ask her pediatrician for another blood draw next week so we can see what her numbers look like. It's frustrating feeling like we've just been left for a month to try to live a normal life when nothing is normal!

Eliza has already graduated out of the Sooner Start program from the state. While I was gone, a therapist and nutritionist came to evaluate Eliza and determined she's well enough to not need Sooner Start. I guess that's a mixed blessing. She could probably use some further treatment, but we're glad she's well enough to not be in dire need.

We had an interesting Thanksgiving. I was welcomed home by Eliza throwing up her feeding tube again and having to reinsert it, while Joel asked me, "Isn't this more fun than Disney World?"

"No, just funnier! I have to laugh sometimes. Otherwise, I'd drown."

Later in the day, Robin leaked through her diaper during naptime and decided to make "art" on the wall and crib. Yes, she rubbed poop every-where! Despite all the scrubbing with a toothbrush and hydrogen peroxide, her hand still stinks! Ah, parenthood—you gotta love it! Apparently, we have an artist on our hands.

We did enjoy a very large and delicious Thanksgiving meal with friends and are very thankful for all that we do have! God is good, all the time. God is good, even when things are a bit scary!

PS: Zoë did toss her cookies on the airplane home— it didn't seem like a big deal at that time, but now she's running a fever. Pray for protection over our family, that we don't all get sick again! Please, no more, Jesus. Not for a while.

Returning home from Florida was a mixed bag for me. I was very happy to be home, but the reality of our continued battle on Eliza's behalf was weighing me down, both physically and spiritually. We had a chart pinned to our refrigerator door that tracked Eliza's daily medications, numbering nine, that she had to take multiple times a day—shots, Nepro strength and time for each meal, blood pressure, weight, and number and weight of each wet diaper. It was exhausting tracking all this with life's daily distractions. How did I think this would be easier than having a full-time nursing staff at the hospital? Instead of three to four eyes on her care, there was just me. My respect for nurses grew two-fold, and my heart ached for other full-time caretakers. It doesn't take long to feel isolated, as leaving the house for normal activities seems impossible, not to mention the cost of increased exhaustion.

A Renewed Battle

Sent: *Tuesday, November 28, 2006, 3:54 p.m.*
Subject: *Tears…*

Here I am again, broken and naked before you, crying out to my Savior for mercy and grace. I feel much like Jesus must have in the garden of Gethsemane, weeping before my Father, asking Him to please let this cup pass from me. I have to trust that He's weeping too, knowing my pain and hurting for me, but knowing what must be done is for the good of our family.

I got the lab results back from Eliza's blood draw yesterday. It pains me to share that Eliza's creatinine has gone up from 1.9 two weeks ago to 2.1. I know this isn't a large increase, but we were hoping that she would have continued on the downward trend (perhaps even be normal again). I do have to bear in mind that her dialysis was cut down by two hours a day, which may be why it has increased. What this may indicate, though, is that her kidneys have hit a plateau. Perhaps this is all the function that is going to return. Is it enough to stop dialysis? I think it's highly unlikely. My mind is racing as the reality of a kidney transplant has slapped me in the face again. I'm overwhelmed by that reality, the need to test family members for a perspective match. What if one of us is a match? That will just be one more person we love undergoing surgery and giving a part of their health.

I'll share this now as the question has surfaced before: no one under the age of eighteen or sixteen (I can't remember now) can donate a kidney. This, thankfully, takes out Robin and Zoë! The blood vessels in children are so small that they need larger vessels from a mature kidney to connect to. They have found the blood flow to be stronger and the success rate to be higher with adult kidneys.

We don't see the nephrologist until next Tuesday, but my hopes of Eliza returning to normal have been shattered. It's been entirely too long without regaining full function. I don't know what they will say next week, but I'm bracing myself for the worst, which in my mind is preparing for transplant. There's a part of me that knows I need to be thankful. Eliza is alive, and I get to enjoy her giggles and warm smiles every day, and yet there's another part of me that says, "This isn't living." I want so much more for her. She's too little to be facing such big things. Three months ago, she was perfectly normal, other than allergies.

Eliza's calcium is still high. I'm waiting to hear back from the doctor about whether or not I can cut back on her calcium carbonate. I pray that will solve some of our issues.

All right, this is all too ironic for me. I just got a phone call from our medical insurance. It was from a lady who will be my contact person should we need to pursue a transplant. She just called to check up on Eliza and asked questions about her current health. She talked me through the entire process of requesting a transplant and the steps taken. Is this part of the preparation, Lord?

Please pray for Joel and me. We're over-whelmed and scared! This is big, and we feel so little. I want to say a huge thank-you to all of you who have donated toward Eliza's medical fund. It goes in anonymously, so I can't thank each of you personally, but I sure wish I could! Thank you, thank you, thank you for supporting us through this very difficult and scary time.

It was about this time that I had my crisis of faith. Late at night, while I tossed in bed, longing for sleep, the enemy entered our room, taunting me with the whisperings of doubt, "What if everything you've ever believed is a lie? What if there isn't a God out there, listening to you? What if Eliza dies? Where will she go? Who will hold you?" Fear washed over me in such powerful waves of anguish that I rolled out of bed and crumpled into a ball on our bedroom floor, rocking with tears. The blackness was real—it engulfed me. I had never been in this place before, where the darkness was palpable and overwhelming. My mind actually went to that place where there is no God, no Savior, no hope, just darkness. Separation. The pain was immense as I wrestled with what I thought I knew. No, I do know it, don't I? Hasn't the Lord been there with me from the very beginning? Did He not heal me in Guatemala? Save me from an early death? I sensed heaven then, felt it, just as real as I'm feeling this darkness now. Hadn't Jesus held me in my dreams as a young girl? Yes! It was so real. It was Him.

Muffled at first, I cried out in my heart, "No, my Savior lives. He's real. Very real...and He is good." I began to recall all the times I had clearly seen His hand in my life, weaving a tapestry according to His design. As my mind recalled each instance, the darkness began to lift bit by bit with each profession *of faith. I found myself standing. "I will not let you steal from me my hope in the one thing that can save me. Jesus! Jesus, come! Fight for me!"*

Now that some time has passed, Revelation 12:11 comes to mind: They triumphed over him (Satan) by the blood of the Lamb and by the word of their testimony; they did not love their lives so much as to shrink from death. I was being empowered by the blood of the Lamb, who took away my sin and sanctified me to Himself. It was the word of my testimony that was giving me strength to stand against the enemy of my soul.

When I was thirteen years old, my family went on a mission trip to Guatemala to minister to a girl's home our church supported. We spent two weeks visiting hospitals, helping with various construction projects at the home, building relationships with the girls abandoned for one reason or another, and sharing the gospel when possible. My heart was so struck by the entire experience I asked my parents if I could return again the following summer with a team from another church.

Wondering if the Lord was calling me toward full-time mission work after graduation, which prompted me to fly out a week prior to the mission team, I spent a week living as one of the girls in the home, sharing their room, food, and school. It was a very lonely and eye-opening week for me. I had a taste of what it was like to not have a parent to call your own, to have to share everything with twenty other girls who harbored jealousies and insecurities of their own.

When the team from California joined me, I was relieved to be back to ministering in the hospitals, nursing homes, and local churches. We spent two weeks doing the same types of activities that I had experienced the prior summer. We spent our last weekend decompressing as a team in the tourist town of Antigua before returning home. Our first morning there, we went to a local bakery for break-fast, after which we planned to explore the area. After eating, I started to feel really strange physically, which led me back to the hotel, where some of our team was enjoying the swimming pool. I sat with them, dangling my feet in the water for a while, before it became obvious I needed to lie down. I ventured back to my shared room alone, weak and spent. It wasn't long before I found myself struggling to breathe, gasping for air. What was happening to me? Not being one to overexaggerate or draw undue attention to myself, I found myself panicked and all alone. I hadn't mentioned to my teammates at the pool how sick I was feeling.

Fearful, I began praying in earnest, "Lord, please send someone to help me! Please, I can't breathe, and I'm so weak I can't get out of bed. I'm scared! Please, help me!" After a few minutes, I saw the outline of one of our local team leaders (an American who lived full-time at the girls' home) walking past my room. I mustered all the strength I could and yelled for her between gasps, "Suzy! Suzy, please help me!" I banged something on the side table to create noise as her outline stopped and turned toward the room door. Thank You, Jesus. *She entered and, seeing me gasping, ran to my bed-side. "What's wrong?"*

"I can't breathe, and I feel terrible!" Seeing the fear in my eyes, she put her hands on me and started praying in rapid-fire Spanish. I didn't understand a word of it but heartily agreed as I regained my breath. After several minutes, she went in search for

others to help. More people on our team entered my room, laying hands on me in prayer.

For the next two hours, I became so cold I had five wool blankets layered on me, while still shaking. I couldn't get warm enough, and yet I was sweating. My fever began to increase from 101 to 104 to 105, which began to greatly concern my team leaders. They had called a local doctor, but since it was raining, he was unwilling to come—not until it had stopped. In great concern to lower my fever, they talked of putting me in a cold bath, to which I begged, "Please no! I'll go into shock, I'm so cold!" I began to feel a tingling sensation in my legs that quickly turned to a complete loss of feeling. Two team members were praying over me, and more were outside, praying together.

I had a cold, wet washcloth on my forehead, covering my eyes. I struggled to hide my tears as I began to wonder if I'd make it home to the States or if I'd end up with paralyzed legs. Why can't I feel them? *I wondered. Through tears I said goodbye to my family in my mind, wishing I could talk to them on the phone but knowing our rooms didn't provide them. My parents had been contacted, but I don't think the team leaders knew what to tell them. "Shannon is sick, but we have a doctor coming, hopefully soon."*

My thinking was becoming fuzzy as the pain in my body grew. I was now begging God to either take me home to be with Him or heal me. "But please don't leave me in this place." As I was praying, an intense sense of peace washed over me. It was as if Jesus were looking down on my bed, inches from me, with His hand outstretched, ready to take me home. Never have I felt what I did in that moment, nor do I expect to again on this side of heaven's door.

I experienced the most peace, love, joy, acceptance, and exhilaration, all tied together, wrapping my soul. I just needed to reach out, and I was sure Jesus would take my hand, but as I was thinking this, the doctor walked in. He took one look at me and panicked. My temperature was now 106 degrees. He quickly went into action, rambling in Spanish as the people in the room scrambled to his every command. He forced a warm Gatorade liquid down my dry throat and turned me over to give me a shot. To this day, I have no idea what the shot contained or its purpose.

More prayer ensued as teams rotated to watch over me. I remember the pain quickly moving to my head—it pounded. Every whisper or creak of a chair sent chills down my spine. Was it possible for one's head to hurt this bad? The light hurt, and my bed grew extremely uncomfortable, but tossing was out of the question due to the pain. Sweating profusely, I clumsily threw blanket after blanket off my sweat-drenched clothes. Sweet sleep wasn't found until the late midnight hours.

The next morning, I awoke feeling the hunger pangs in my stomach, and sat up abruptly to assess the room; there was a teammate asleep on a chair across the room, but no one else. What time is it? Where is everyone? Did they leave for breakfast without me? How long have I been sleeping? Hours? Days? What have I missed? *I bounced out of bed to inspect, waking the chair-sleeper. "Shannon, are you all right? What are you doing out of bed?"*

"What? Why? I feel great. Where is everyone? I'm starved. Is it time for breakfast?"

Jaw dropping, my teammate looked me up and down. "Are you sure you feel all right? You moaned a lot in your sleep last night. Maybe you should sit down. Does your head still hurt?"

"No, I feel fine, really. Nothing hurts. I'm hungry." I opened the room door and looked down the corridor. Noticing I was still wearing yesterday's clothes, I stepped out and knocked on the neighboring door, looking for everyone else. The gal opening the door stared at me in shocked surprise.

"Shannon! What are you doing out of bed?"

"I'm hungry. Are you guys getting breakfast soon? Can I go with you?"

After some hesitant laughter, the room erupted with activity, everyone talking at once, hugging me. I began to hear from each of them how sick I had been and how frightened they were for me. "I never left the outside of your room yesterday, praying for you," one man ventured.

"Well, I feel great! Let's eat!"

I was a typical fourteen-year-old, hungry and ready to go, not fully grasping yet the seriousness of the situation for all the adults in the room who were in charge of my care. Walking to breakfast, they took turns looking at me with profound wonder as one looks upon a walking miracle.

Apparently, the Lord chose to heal me rather than take me home, but I still hold tightly to the "whiff" of heaven Jesus granted me. Whatever happened in that moment before the doctor arrived was real. Very, very real. And I praise the Lord for giving me a glimpse of what is to come, if you can even call it a glimpse, as I didn't see anything, just felt it. I tell my girls, "If that was just a glimpse, I'm telling you, that's where I'm going. That's worth anything on this side of heaven's gates, as Paul said in Romans 8:18, 'I consider that our present sufferings are not worth comparing with the glory that will be revealed in us.""

In my early childhood, my parents struggled in their marriage, as most do with the mounting pressures of the world apart from Jesus. My mom struggled with undiagnosed depression that led her to episodes of sporadic behavior and long naps. But the Lord, who is always drawing, had a plan. My dad has shared that it was while attending a family funeral and witnessing the fellowship among church members that he began to question who would help them in a time of crisis. Who were their fellowship? Of course, they had great friends with whom they enjoyed combined vacations and activities, but it was different from a church family who could care for your needs.

This conundrum led my parents to seek out a church when I was very young. So as long as I can remember, I've attended church. But things at home were still difficult. The mounting pressures led my parents to argue frequently and created an unsettling culture in our home, as divorce seemed highly possible. I also had several learning disabilities.

When I was in kindergarten, I was tested for learning disabilities, leading to years of special ed. I had dyslexia, sensory integration problems, and a speech impediment that made the letter r torture to pronounce. I was known to walk into walls or veer while walking due to the sensory integration struggle—my brain had a hard time processing audiovisual input, causing me to appear "slow."

From my earliest years, I spent half my school day seeing specialists outside the classroom—speech therapy, occupational therapy, and special ed. This led to bullying, as I was an easy target. One muddy morning, while I was waiting in line to enter our classroom, a boy pushed me into a mud puddle, laughing as he did so. I sat in the nurse's office, dripping in mud, waiting for clean clothes from home. Another time, a girl put a paper bag on my head and told me I was so ugly no one should have to look at me. In high school, this girl got saved and the Lord had us minister together after Joel and I were married. She is now a dear friend and sister in Christ! During a group project, I was told to just write the names on the paper since I was too dumb to help with anything else. School was a struggle. I had friends, but I was also the brunt of many jokes, whisperings, and being outrightly stereotyped.

Because of the severity of my dyslexia, I was told early on that college would likely be unattainable. But my parents were never ones to take things lying down, leading them to find alternative therapies. I started sound therapy during my sleep. For years, I listened to classical music with sound variations intertwined to create new pathways in my brain. By the time I was in sixth grade, to my special ed teacher's delight and surprise, I tested out of the special ed program. I entered junior high on my own—no outside help. I struggled, never getting above a B-/C average, but I was doing it alone! When it came time for college, I was determined to prove to myself that I could do it! And I did! I got my first 4.0 my fourth year in college, the first semester Joel and I were married, no less! Married and a 4.0, not to mention an invitation to the honor roll!

Because of the brokenness at home, having my naivete taken advantage of physically by a neighbor boy, and the hardships at school, I carried a sadness in my heart. It was during this time that I had a recurring dream. It was always the same; a massive, full tree whose branches bowed from the weight of its lushness stood rooted next to a rushing stream. Lounging against its trunk was a man, glowing white. I don't remember His face, just radiating light, filled with joy and love. In my dream, I'd crawl into this man's lap and rest my head against His chest as He held me all night, engulfed in love and peace. I remember always waking feeling refreshed and loved, very, very loved. I knew my parents loved me, but this was a love that couldn't be explained in human terms. Now, as an adult, it's easy to look back and recognize it was Jesus holding me in my dreams. He met me, a hurting little girl, in the sweetness of my dreams, reminding me that Jesus is always with me.

When I was about eight years old, the fighting between my parents hit a fever pitch. The night finally came when the escalation caused my mother to leave in a rage of tears as my sister and I crawled into my bed together, clinging to each other for comfort through our tears. Would she come back? Where did she go? We were confused but figured this moment would eventually come, as divorce seemed imminent. I will never forget my dad entering our dark room and sitting on the side of the bed. "Girls, I want you to know that no matter what happens between me and Mom, I will always take care of you. I love you and will always be here for you."

The next afternoon, after returning from school, we heard my mom's voice. It was coming from the master bedroom. No, wait. Could it be? Yes, it was definitely her and my father—they were talking, not yelling. They were crying together. What did this mean? We tiptoed into the room, not wanting to break what was happening. Through tearstained faces, they both smiled at us. Yes, Mom would be staying, and they were committed to getting marriage counseling.

The night before, after my mom left our house in a cloud of uncertainty, she drove close to one hundred miles from Boulder to Colorado Springs. My father was distraught, not knowing where she went. To muddy waters, the cause of her own mother's death the year before remained uncertain. My grandmother, also battling depression, had died in a horrible car accident, driving full speed into a cement overpass column on I-25 in Denver. The question lingered whether she had steered intentionally into the column or had fallen asleep at the wheel. Fear gripped my father. Phyllis wouldn't do anything irrational, would she? *he probably thought. He made several unsuccessful phone calls seeking her, including her father and their pastor.*

The next morning, word came from their pastor, Dr. Bob. "Rich, Phyllis called and asked to meet with me. She spent the night in a hotel in Colorado Springs."

"I don't know what can be done for her or our marriage. It's hopeless at this point."

"Now, don't get hasty. Let me spend some time with her and we'll see."

During that meeting, our pastor led my mother to the Lord. For the first time, she experienced the freedom of forgiveness and the power of the Spirit to bring change from within. When she returned home to my father, he couldn't believe the instant change he saw in her. There was a peace and new resolve to move forward with Jesus in their marriage. They started seeing a counselor, who diagnosed my mother's clinical depression and helped her get the medical care needed.

Over the course of the next several weeks, I began to see a major change in my mother. She was no longer unpredictable in her reactions to everyday situations, and I observed her studying her Bible regularly. There was new peace that had washed over her and our home. Jesus had changed her, and it encouraged me greatly. Marriage counseling also greatly improved my parents' relationship, bringing a new peace. The Lord was doing a work in our home, and to this day, I praise Him for it!

*****

Sent*: Tuesday, December 5, 2006, 4:33 p.m.*
Subject*: Well…*

Um, strange doctor's appointment today. The bottom line is this: Eliza's creatinine went up again from 2.1 to 2.4, and her pee output has decreased over the past two weeks from the 500cc range to the 300cc range, which, combined, may mean her kidneys are starting to deteriorate. It's probable they were doing their best to regain function but due to the amount of damage, they can't sustain it. Her doctor (one of the three nephrologists at Children's we see) wants to give Eliza another month before we make any big decisions regarding long-term care— i.e. transplant. It has been three months without her regaining full function, which is not good, but she wants to be certain that she's not going to regain more before proceeding with a transplant. There would have to be a dramatic turnaround in order to avoid it, which means regaining full function, for which if she hasn't by now, medically speaking, her chances are slim to none. The doctor said, "In my opinion, transplant is on the road ahead, but I want to give it a little more time." The doctors want to be very sure. I have peace in knowing they don't take it lightly.

So in the meantime, we sit tight, try to live, try to come to terms with where God has us, and pray, pray, pray. Good news: Eliza's hemoglobin is good enough that they cut back on her Procrit shots for another two weeks, and then we only have to give it to her once a week instead of twice. They also cut back on the dosage of her blood pressure medicine. Otherwise, things stay the same.

My second appointment with the GI doctor didn't produce much. She said it's quite common for children on tube feedings to throw up in the mornings if they're fed at night. So she has cut Eliza off all nighttime feedings. Praise God! No more getting up in the middle of the night to start her machine! Our nutritionist also cut back on the amount of food Eliza gets each day. So we are to give her three smaller feedings per day. Hopefully, this will help. She said there's no guarantee that Eliza will stop throwing up in the morning since it may be caused by the dialysis, but at least she won't be losing calories or nutrition. We have been giving her antinausea medications, and if they aren't preventing her from vomiting, then she may just need to do it regardless. There aren't any other medications she can prescribe to help at this point.

We also talked about trying to wean off the tube feedings. I'm not sure I'm ready just yet, but I'm going to keep the instructions at hand—perhaps next week. The nutritionist told me that sometimes patients don't get their appetite or desire for food back until after a transplant since dialysis tends to make food taste strange. She may just need to be tube-fed until then, which according to her is not such a bad thing, since they really want to monitor your nutrition and weight level prior to surgery.

I find myself singing along with Rich Mullins, "If I stand, let me stand on the promise that you will pull me through and if I can't, let me fall on the grace that first brought me to you."[18]

Pray with us, that we would continue to stand on the promises of God regardless of what we see. As I've said before, His character has not changed just because our life circumstances have.

"Though I walk in the midst of trouble, You preserve my life; You stretch out Your hand against the anger of my foes, with Your right hand You saved me. The Lord will fulfill His purposes for me; Your love, O Lord, endures forever—do not abandon the works of Your hands" (Ps. 137:7–8).

We are still in the midnight hour; anything could happen, but we're still standing.

December 5, 2006, is etched in my memory as one of the lowest moments in my Eliza journey, as my fears were confirmed. The door in my mind I had covered in caution tape—TRANSPLANT: DON'T TOUCH—was being forced open yet again. Lord, why can't I have peace about the idea of a transplant? Surely, people have them all the time, so why is it such a hard concept for me? Give me peace, please! I had figured all along that if we should have to go through that door, the Lord would take my hand, put it on the handle, and help me turn it. But here I sat in the nephrologist office, feeling completely alone, not abandoned, but alone, facing my fears; it was as if Jesus was willing me to continue to hope for something that seemed medically impos-

---

[18] Rich Mullins, "If I Stand," in *Winds of Heaven, Stuff of Earth* (Tennessee: Reunion Records, 1988).

sible. The internal battle was immense as the doctor was basically giving me a month to come to terms with Eliza's condition. Haven't I been holding on, Lord? And weren't we seeing glimpses of recovery? For what? For Eliza to ultimately need a transplant? Help me. I'm drowning and just want Your will to be done, regardless of the outcome. If it's to be transplant, then give me Your peace that surpasses all understanding. If it's to be recovery, then again, give me Your peace. I'm longing for You, regardless. At this point, since You still haven't given me peace about transplant, or permission in my heart to accept it, I'm going to continue looking to You. I'm going to continue coming to You on Eliza's behalf like the persistent widow. Please, Jesus, let her life be found in You and You alone and not dependent on any machine or transplant. You are her Father, and You are the one who holds her days. Your will be done. I'm trusting You will give me the grace to accept it either way.

*****

Sent: *Saturday, December 16, 2006, 11:09 a.m.*
Subject: *Quick update*

Started writing on Thursday, December 14:

I realized this morning that it's been a while since I've written, and I should send out a quick update. We have gotten caught up in the business of the Christmas season—i.e., getting presents finished and in the mail, preparing for fun parties, getting our tree up (which took us a week: first, the tree, then the lights, then the ornaments), but it's beautiful and reminds us of how trees paved much of our spiritual heritage, from the fall in the garden of Eden to Noah's ark, the cradle Jesus lay in, and most importantly, the cross.

Eliza is doing well. We are still battling with throw-up. On occasion we have a day lapse, but overall, it's continuous. We have just come to accept it and really to expect it as well. We have become pretty "quick draws" with the throw-up bucket!

We do have a praise report! Eliza is now officially off all blood pressure medications! We are still in shock and confusion about this. How is that possible since your kidneys help regulate your blood pressure? Doesn't make sense, but we are thrilled! Even with her off the medications, her blood pressure has been super low, at times too low. Two days ago, I had to call the nephrologist since her BP was only 67/48 (low range for a child her age is 75/50). She looked fine, but it concerned me. They told me to give her three ounces of water through her nose tube and then check again in a half-hour. It went back up to 95/57—perfect! So given the information, we are running our own experiment. We have decided to give her three ounces of water at six o'clock each morning in hopes that will raise her blood pressure before she feeds at 8:00 a.m. and starts moving around. We are wondering if she's throwing up due to low BP in the morning. Yesterday was the first trial day, and it worked. We'll see about today!

I think I've given up trying to "figure out" Eliza's overall health. It's not worth the mental energy since she changes way too much and often quickly. Her pee output has gone back up, but I don't know if that means anything. I'm only keeping track so I have something to show the nephrologist at our next appointment. Oh, and since she's off BP medicine, she only has to take three medications twice a day! That's a far cry from the six to seven she came home with.

Eliza made the Oklahoman newspaper again yesterday. Joel's work is doing a raffle drawing for a 2006 OU football signed by Adrian Peterson and Bob Stoops. It has become quite an event! I'm taking Eliza into Joel's office next Friday to draw the winning name. A huge thank-you to all of you locally who have been selling or buying tickets—we are blown away by the amount of support and care on our behalf!

The Lord has been teaching me about the art of "centering." What do I mean by that? Scripture tells us that God is like a potter and we are like the clay in His hands. We can either be elastic and pliable in our Father's hands, or we can resist Him and make it hard to be formed. Interestingly, I took a wheel-throwing class in college that now has a whole new meaning to me. See, Dad, it wasn't a waste of money! Plus, you got some pretty funny-looking bowls. Wink, wink. Yes, my bowls were terrible, and the vases even worse. Why? Because I never learned the art of "centering" my clay. In order to throw a beautiful piece of artwork, you have to have the clay perfectly centered on the wheel; otherwise, you end up with a wonky, off-centered object. You can usually mask this defect by making small or thick pieces of artwork. They are functional, just not always attractive or practical. This was how I managed to squeak through my class, but my professor was far from impressed.

In order to center your clay, you have to apply a ton of pressure while gently pushing the clay toward the center of the wheel. It can be physically difficult and frustrating, depending on the clay. I realize this is the same with the Lord; He has to center us before He can pull us into a piece of artwork. "You turn things upside down, as if the potter were thought to be like the clay! Shall what is formed say to Him who formed it, 'He did not make me?' Can the pot not say of the potter, 'He knows nothing?'" (Isa. 29:16). The hardest and most painful part of making pottery is centering the clay; it's tedious and challenging, but once complete, there are no limits to what can be formed.

God has to center us before He can throw us. Much like a potter, He has to apply a great amount of pressure in order to guide us toward the center of His will. But as clay, we can either be pliable or stiff—it's up to us. After we're centered, then God can begin to form us according to His plan. He may choose to make us into a simple serving bowl (one that the cat drinks from) or an intricate vase (one that sits in the presidential hall)—it's all the work of His hands and for His glory so that none could boast! We may even end up being formed into several different pieces of artwork over our lifetime. The potter always reserves the right to throw the clay back onto the wheel.

Once clay is soft, centered, and formed according to the potter's will, it then must enter the fire— another painful but very necessary process to burn off the deformities and harden the clay for use.

Today, I pray that I may be pliable and easy to work with as the Lord has His way, forming me according to His will. May I enter the fire with grace and thanksgiving, knowing I will have a function on the other side, all for the Potter's glory. I look forward to seeing what He is making me into.

*****

Picked back up on Saturday, December 16:

I have lost track of time! I just don't seem able to keep up with myself. I'm bummed to share that our experiment with Eliza's feedings has failed. She threw up all over her changing table yesterday after I took her BP, which was perfect! Which makes me conclude that she's not throwing up because her BP is low. Regardless of what we do, she is continually throwing up at least once a day. Perhaps it's just as simple as "she is on dialysis." The poor, poor baby. I know it bothers me more than her. I hate seeing her like this, and I'm tired of having such an intimate relationship with our wet vac! It's probably the best investment we've made all year.

I had a pair of favorite black pants I wore to the hospital almost daily during Eliza's six-week stay, mostly because they were as comfortable as my pajama pants but looked nice. I was determined to not dress frumpy going to the hospital, even though it would have been easy to do, as we spent a lot of our time sitting at Eliza's bedside. It was one way I could keep my life somewhat normal, getting up in the morning, going through my usual routine, showering and dressing for the day. I would listen to worship music while showering, which usually led to torrents of tears. It always felt really good to get it all out in the presence of the Lord before the day and new battles began.

Around mid-December, my black pants were taking a hit from so much use, so I ventured to a local consignment shop in search of a replacement. As I was looking through the racks, my heart stopped as I came to a purple shirt. Could it be? Oh, my! It's my size! It was a velvet shirt with a ribbon-covered V-neck from my favorite name brand. I received their catalog in our junk mail every couple of months and usually just drooled over the items I liked, knowing they were out of reach financially. There was one particular shirt I had made note of in the previous catalog, longing for it but again knowing it wasn't possible at eighty-five dollars. But here right in front of me was that very shirt, in my size, for only seven dollars! I pulled it out, gently running my finger along the ribbon as my heart burst with the overwhelming sense that Jesus was winking at me. My heart was greatly encouraged; He was the only one who knew my desire for that shirt, and yet out of love, He had placed it here for me, brand-new, never worn, for only seven dollars. Oh, how He loves me and shows me in such intimate ways His gentle care for even silly things, like desired shirts.

*****

Sent: *Friday, December 22, 2006, 4:28 p.m.*
Subject: *Hearts full of thanksgiving*

Wow! What an exciting day for us! This morning, at Joel's work, Eliza drew the winning name of the signed Bob Stoops / Adrian Peterson OU football. To our surprise, it goes to Mr. Bowls from our church! We didn't rig anything, I promise! In fact, you can see for yourselves, as the drawing will be aired on both Channel 5 and Channel 9 News tonight. We were shocked and amazed how much money was raised on Eliza's behalf. Are you ready? Drumroll, please...close to $11,000! I don't even think I can say it out loud, as I'm still in shock. Thank you, thank you, thank you to all who helped with this fundraiser, either by selling or buying tickets. I can hardly believe it! We promise to put the money to *good use toward Eliza's growing health needs! We are so appreciative—what can one say? I'm actually at a loss for words.*

I'm beaming, as I have another big *praise! Eliza's GI doctor has prescribed a new antacid, which so far seems to have stopped her throwing up. I almost don't want to say that out loud, but we are on day 3 without having to use the wet vac or paper towels to clean our walls. What a Christmas present for me, literally and figuratively! May this be the start of a full recovery for Eliza!*

Wow! My heart is overjoyed! Oh, Eliza extended her arms to be held by the reporter and cameraman after the raffle. I believe she made their days! The cameraman from Channel 9 stayed around after everyone else left, to play his Indian flute for us. He said, "Sometimes when I get really inspired by a story I'm doing, I like to play my flute for people." The girls love it, and Zoë got more excited to play her recorder.

Merry Christmas! Hug yourselves for me. Now go and hug someone else for me!

Emmanuel—God With Us

Sent: *Sunday, December 24, 2006, 2:23 p.m.*
Subject: *Blessings continue*

Wow! There are so many caring people out there—I had no idea! We were doorbell-ditched last night as someone left a huge bag of Christmas presents for the girls. They don't even know our girls' names; they left a card that says, "Please accept these gifts from our family to yours. May your family be blessed this holiday season and through the year. Our prayers are with you and your family during this difficult time. I apologize we don't know the names of your children, so we placed tags with a #4 for your four-year-old daughter, and twin 1 and twin 2 for the twins. Merry Christmas!"

I'm still in awe. I'm learning from these wonderful people about reaching out in love to others who are hurting in our community. Even if I don't know them by name! It was fun for me to hear giggling outside and car doors slamming after I answered the doorbell and saw the bag. They were sure having fun, and boy, do we feel blessed!

My heart is full as I see people, mostly strangers, surrounding us during this time. God came down to meet us in the same way two thousand years ago. Christmas has a whole new meaning to us this year. Without Jesus, there would be no hope for Eliza's healing. We are clinging to that!

I feel like that woman who followed closely after Jesus in the crowd, longing just to touch the hem of His robe. If only I could reach it; if only I knew where Jesus was and I could drive, fly, or run the distance to find Him. I would go any length on Eliza's behalf. But that's the crazy thing—He's already here! At any time, on any given day, I can reach out and touch the hem of His robe through prayer and know that He's going to turn to see me. He has seen, He has heard, He is answering, all because He chose to come as a baby on Christmas morning. Wow! What an amazing and humbling truth!

Eliza asked to eat some soup today for lunch. I was shocked, as she kept asking for more. She ate at least ten bites and kept it down!! This is the most food she has eaten by mouth since being in the hospital, which was a Braum's hamburger around her birthday, two months ago. Perhaps now that she's not throwing up as much, her interest in food is increasing? Praise God! I've never been so excited to see a kid eat before! Plus, she asked for it!! If things continue on this path, I think I'll try to wean her off the feeding tube this next week by cutting her Nepro intake in half. I've been told it could take up to a month to completely wean her, but I think it may finally be time to start—it's almost too good to be true.

Have a "Mary Christmas," resting at the feet of Jesus.

Hours after sending this e-mail, we tucked the girls in for the night. It was bittersweet to be celebrating Christmas without family. Typically, we celebrate with my parents, but they had spent so much time at our home they rightfully felt the need to be with my sister's family and my brother in Colorado. The loneliness tugged at my heart as nothing felt right.

We prepared the girls' Christmas stockings and settled in for the night, longing for rest after a full day at church and the excitement of Eliza eating her first bites of real food in months. I was also processing what a friend had told me at church. "We had a family member who was healed on Christmas." *Oh, for that to be true for Eliza! Lord, let it be so! I know it's not a matter of ability—You could take this all away in a moment. It's a matter of Your will, as You long to mold us into Your image. Though outwardly we are wasting away, inwardly we are being renewed day by day. Thank You for that truth!*

After wrestling to find sleep, in the wee hours of the morning, we heard an obnoxious alarm coming from the twins' room. Running, in hopes of quieting the noise to preserve the girls' sleep, we noticed the electricity was off. *Oh no! The alarm is letting us know there's no power running to the dialysis machine! No dialysis means no help for Eliza's kidneys! How long can she go like that?*

We tried so hard not to fret, but with the power out, we had no phone service—meaning, we couldn't reach anyone to ask for help. I spent time in fretful prayer before the Lord again, repeating what I had written to family. *Where are You? I'll go anywhere just to touch the hem of Your robe! Please, Jesus, where are You? I'm begging again for You to heal Eliza. I pray her life wouldn't be dependent on a machine for life, but rather dependent on You alone! I'm here, in the dark, begging! Like the persistent widow in Luke, I'm not leaving until I hear from You!*

In the silence of Christmas morning, as the world slept, the Lord impressed on my heart my own written words. "I have seen you, I have heard you." *But nothing has changed, Lord! She's stuck to a machine! Please! Free her! Let this cup pass from her!* "Trust Me. I'm here. I am Emmanuel, God with you."

This response sent me to my knees in stunned reverence. *Yes, yes, You are Emmanuel. You are here with us.* The reality that I was begging for God's presence in the wee hours of the morning of the day we celebrate His entering the world—*our* world—coming to us as a babe, divesting Himself of all the privileges and riches of heaven to walk this life with us, to bear our brokenness and sin, struck me dumb. That the Lord, "who being in very nature God, did not consider equality with God something to be used to his own advantage; rather, he made Himself nothing by taking the very nature of a servant, being made in human likeness. And being found in appearance as a man, he humbled Himself by becoming obedient to death—even death on a cross!" (Phil. 2:6–8).

Never has Emmanuel meant more to me, or been more real. A peace washed over me, that no matter what happened with Eliza, we had Emmanuel, and that truth could never be taken from us. He would continue to see us through, walking by our side and empowering us with His grace moment by moment.

The girls woke up early, much to our chagrin. Robin and Zoë were up bounding around the Christmas tree, while Eliza whimpered from her room. She was tethered to her machine, like a dog restrained by its leash. She wanted to be with her sisters—and rightfully so! Because we knew Eliza would be tethered until lunchtime, we began bringing Christmas to the twins' room, beginning with their stockings. Robin and Zoë twirled around the room in childish delight, while Eliza watched in a daze. Every attempt to twirl tangled her further in tubing, creating frustration. Oh, how I wanted to set her free from that wretched machine!

Lunch finally arrived, and I set Eliza in her high chair, handing her a few Cheerios, still unsure of her eating habits. She played with a few and slowly began to eat them, one at a time. Turning from the other side of the kitchen, I looked at her in surprise. More real food! Yes! But just as I was thinking this, I witnessed something awesome. Right there, in my kitchen, the very place where Eliza's illness originated, I saw her dingy yellow eyes, which for months had shown the evidence of illness, turn crystal clear.

Eliza has beautiful, teardrop-shaped eyes; they have always been one of her distinguishing features, with bright, clear whites and striking hazel pupils with green undertones. I hadn't seen those brilliant eyes for months, and yet there they were, staring back at me, as if they had never left. *What is happening?* "I am here—Emmanuel."

Later that afternoon, we went to our pastor's house to have dinner with his family. He still, to this day, recalls with delight Eliza meandering with renewed energy through their living room with a piece of turkey sticking out of her mouth. She didn't really eat it as much as she just liked having it in her mouth, but at this point, who cares? The action encouraged our hearts. Something was happening.

> **Sent**: *Wednesday, December 27, 2006, 9:04 a.m.*
> **Subject**: *Prayer request*

> *It's with anticipation that I write this e-mail. I think today is the day, but I'm nervous. Eliza has been doing so well she has not thrown up since we started giving her the new antacid. Well, I take that back; she did throw up once, but we later discovered her pill on the floor by her bed. She must have taken it out of her mouth after Joel left her room. So now Joel sits by her until he's sure it's completely dissolved in her mouth.*

> *Sunday, Christmas Eve day, Eliza ate more food than we've seen her eat since she was in the hospital, around the beginning of October. She actually started asking me for food! I almost fell over when she not only asked for it but also ate it! My girl? Can this be? Eliza, are you feeling all right? She ate food not only at lunch but also again at dinner. Wow! What a Christmas present, huh? She has continued to ask for food since then and has kept it down. Don't get me wrong—she hasn't eaten a ton of food, just small bites, but it's the fact that her interest has returned. Before, we'd offer her food and she'd turn her head away in disgust. Just the sight of food often made her fussy.*

> *So this gets back to my prayer request. I am going to go ahead and take a leap of faith here and start the weaning process today. I'm nervous and really don't want to create a backset for Eliza, but for some reason, it just feels right. The nutritionist*

told me at our last appointment that if I should want to wean her, to start by cutting the Nepro intake in half for a few days and then see how much food she'll eat. If in a few days she's not eating very much, go back to full strength. Please pray that Eliza eats food over the next few days! Pray that she remembers how to chew her food and swallow it without difficulty. Again, I'm nervous, as this feels like a big deal to me, but if we could get her eating before our next appointment on January 9, I'd be thrilled!

I also cut out another one of Eliza's medications. She was on a second antinausea medication that I just felt like she didn't need any more. I sure hope that's the case!

We had a good Christmas—although, very interesting and different. Our power went out around two o'clock Christmas morning and didn't come back on until 5:00 a.m. This, of course, meant that Eliza's dialysis machine was off during that time. When the power came back on, we got to wish our dialysis nurse a very early "Merry Christmas! What do we do?" We had to reprogram the machine, and poor Eliza was stuck on dialysis until eleven o'clock the next morning. We were very glad we opened presents Christmas Eve instead of planning on it in the morning. The girls got to open their stockings in the twins' bedroom, but poor Eliza was very fussy and frustrated that she was tethered. She wanted to run and spin with her sisters!

Sent: *Saturday, December 30, 2006, 9:56 a.m.*
Subject: *Could it be…?*

As I write this, know there is a twinkle in my eye, but my face and voice are very reserved. It's hard to get excited about our ups when downs are always sure to follow. But then again, the day will come when all this shall come to an end—I know that and have great faith in this fact.

So Eliza is doing awesome! She has continued to eat food without much problem. I find her wandering around the kitchen, looking for things to eat and asking me for food. She literally ran to her high chair yesterday and the day before. As of last week, it was a battle just to get her to sit with family in the high chair during mealtime, which was a source of frustration for all of us. But a new Eliza is emerging! Her eyes look brighter, and her demeanor is happy. Although she gets grumpy from hunger pangs that she has to relearn how to respond to. She's had constant food in her stomach for over three months, making these sensations new to her. We're treating her like a six-month-old baby by feeding her mashed-up food until she seems more at ease with chewing and swallowing, but she is doing really well in that regard. She is also drinking like a fiend! She typically carries her sippy cup around for comfort, taking very few sips each day, but the past few days, she has guzzled water as if she hasn't had anything to drink in months. We've been monitoring how much fluid she's getting each day between the sippy cup and the Nepro, and here's the really interesting thing: according to our record keeping, she's peeing out more than she's taking in. What does that mean? We still have no idea—perhaps nothing, but we're sure happy to see it.

Last month, they tested Eliza's dialysis solution to determine how much creatinine was in it, which gives them an idea of how efficient her dialysis program is. They determined based on those numbers that things shouldn't be changed in terms of the number of hours she's on dialysis. It appeared that her dialysis program was right where it needed to be. So that's why it's hard to know if her peeing more means anything or not. My heart is reserved, but I'm so hopeful that God is intervening! It would have to be Him at this point, since she was truly deteriorating last month. Healing or no healing, He's here; I'm sure of it!

The doctor once told me in the hospital (way back in October), after I asked her what we were looking for, "Nothing in particular. When they are getting better, you just know. They look better, and their interest in food comes back. There are no tests that determine when or if that will happen—it just does." So is this what we're seeing? At that time, I remember being frustrated by this comment since it's really not definitive. But now, I think we're starting to see what she meant—Eliza is doing better! Her eyes just look so much bigger and brighter to me.

Pray for my patience. I really want to take her feeding tube out and give it a shot for a day or two to see how she does without any Nepro. Since her interest and appetite are back, I figure, Why not? But thankfully, I have a patient, loving husband who knows a thing or two about rehab medicine. He wants to give her a few more days, but oh, I'm so anxious to see my baby's face again without that nose tube! Now I'm crying. It's been so long since I've seen her face without any tape. She's changed and grown under there, and I long to see it once again as God intended—free and clear. Oh, Lord, help me to be patient!

Teary eyed and full of hope,
Shannon

Now faith is being sure of what we *hope* for and *certain* of what we do not see (Heb. 11:1).

Thank you, thank you for your prayers! If I could give each of you a hug of appreciation, I would! They mean so much to us.

> **Sent**: *Friday, January 5, 2007, 9:30 a.m.*
> **Subject**: *Happy New Year!*
>
> *Happy New Year from the Schulz home! The year 2007 has already proven to be a good year for us!*
>
> *Eliza is officially weaned from her feeding tube! That's right; she's eating table food again! On January 1, Eliza's nose tape was in need of replacing, but Joel and I were both being lazy about fixing it. As Eliza was climbing onto the couch later that afternoon, she got her nose tube caught somehow, and it pulled out. "Oh, darn, I guess we'll just have to see how she does!" She has been eating regular food since and drinking lots of water. In fact, our homeware supply company came last night to pick up her feeding machine and extra supplies, so it's official. Should she need to tube-feed again, we'll have to go through the approval process once again with the insurance company.*
>
> *Eliza's pee output is up and down, up and down, up and all around. It's anyone's guess, really. What does it mean? Anything? Just because Eliza is eating again doesn't mean her kidney function has changed any. In fact, what we've concluded is this: once her doctor changed her acid reflux medicine, she stopped throwing up and her appetite returned. So perhaps that was all it was from the beginning— she didn't want to eat since it would cause her reflux to act up. However, we also believe it was her feeding tube that was irritating her stomach and causing the reflux; it was a nasty cycle. In another week*

or so, we may try taking her off the acid reflux medicine to see how she does. She may not need it now that the tube is gone.

Oh! It's so good to see my baby's face again! I can't tell you how freeing that is for me. She looks like a normal two-year-old again, and her face has changed. She still pointed to her back in the morning, waiting for me to pin the feeding tube to the back of her shirt. I have to remind her that the tube is gone by having her touch her own nose. Once she remembers, she smiles. Such simple sweetness.

Next week is a big week for us. Monday morning, we see Eliza's neurologist for a follow-up appointment to make sure her brain is back up to speed. I don't imagine anything will come from that appointment—she's doing great! But maybe they will see something I've missed. Wednesday is a big day as we venture back into the dialysis until another follow-up appointment. We are seeing yet again another doctor! There are three nephrologists that work at Children's, and they rotate working in the dialysis unit each month. So we're on month 3 since discharge, which means doctor number 3. The challenge with this: each doctor comes with a different perspective, and sometimes they contradict each other. I truly don't know what to expect—the lab results are always the ultimate judge of Eliza's condition.

Please keep us in your prayers, that we would have peace regardless of the outcome of these appointments. Pray that we wouldn't give these doctors more authority than they have. God is the ultimate authority on Eliza's condition. Pray that we would remember that. But also pray that we would make wise decisions, as it may be time to pursue the trans-

plant wait list—we do have everything ready, as requested.

Enjoying new beginnings,
Shannon

On New Year's Day, when Eliza's nose tube came out, the Lord impressed on my heart, "I make all things new. This is a new year and the start of something new. Forget the former things; do not dwell on the past. See, I am doing a new thing! Now it springs up; do you not perceive it? I am making a way in the wilderness and streams in the wasteland" (Isa. 43:18–19).

I didn't know yet what that meant, but I was ever hopeful that something was happening!

New Beginnings

Sent: *Wednesday, January 10, 2007, 3:20 p.m.*
Subject: *Put on your dancing shoes*

It's time to dance before our King, Jesus Christ, the one who is able to do much more than we could ever ask or imagine! He has done it again. I ask, What is impossible with our God? I have found again and again in my life that the answer is a resounding nothing!

The tears are coming, and I haven't even started this e-mail. I'm totally beside myself as we have just witnessed a miracle. Eliza's lab work this morning was nothing short of miraculous—the doctor himself even used those words more than once. He was stunned and short on words, as he didn't even know what to say. He told me that he's never heard of or had a patient recover this far out. He commented, "This will certainly change the way I care for my patients." Really, in my mind the worst thing a doctor can do to a parent is rob them of the hope that their child will recover. Hopefully, he saw today that science and statistics are no match for the hope and grace of our God. In life or death, we always have hope in our Lord! But I'm getting ahead of myself.

Are you ready for the news? Eliza's creatinine was down to 1.1; her phosphorus and calcium levels were normal. Normal, I tell you! And that's after eating table food for ten days! Her BUN last month was 78, but it has dropped dramatically to 21 today, close to normal (10–18). I can hardly believe it! Here is the most exciting news of all: Eliza is to go off dialysis until Monday to see how she does! On Monday, we'll have another blood draw to see how her body is handling itself without external help. As long as her creatinine remains below 2.0, she will stay off dialysis. However, if it should go up, she will be put back on for less time—perhaps seven hours a day or four days a week. Her hemoglobin was also remarkable, really high at 15.3, which has prompted them to cut off all her Procrit shots until her lab work shows otherwise. Oh, darn, no more shots or dialysis! Can it be? Will our life pick up where it left off in September?

Dancing before the eternal throne,
Shannon

E-mail Responses

This is the best news I have heard in a long time. I cannot explain how happy I am to hear this. Only God has such miraculous powers. He is truly the King of Kings.

I'm bawling like a baby while reading this on my phone. The power of prayer never stops to amaze me.

Praise God! What an awesome testimony of how God still answers prayers!

I'm *so* excited! God is so incredible! He is so awesome! He never comes too late. Wow! I'm just speechless.

All afternoon, I received continuous e-mails of praise and admiration for our Lord! I thought my heart might burst from the joy! He was and is worthy of all the praise He can receive! It was a glimpse of the day that will come when every knee will bow, in heaven and on earth and under the earth (Phil. 2:10); we will be so taken with His majesty there will be no other response but to fall on our knees. What other response could there be?

I admit, I went into this doctor's appointment with great apprehension clothed in hope. We were seeing the one doctor who, from the beginning, had written Eliza off as a transplant patient and had slowly been trying to prepare me for it; he was just doing his job, which I'm thankful for, but also held tightly to the fact that Jesus was the ultimate authority, not him.

Before we saw him, labs were drawn, and I had time to share with our dialysis nurse all the things we were seeing—the clearing of her eyes, returned desire for food, increased pee output, overall increase in energy, etc. It all had me wondering, "What do you think? Is it possible she's getting better?"

"I don't know, but the labs will tell us." Stepping away, she said she'd ask the doctor what he thought. *Oh, I'm sure I already know what he thinks. Lord, help me. I'm not crazy, am I?* Returning a few minutes later, she laughed. "Well, he laughed that off. He thinks she's too far gone to be anything other than a transplant patient. Remember, if function doesn't return in a month, it's increasingly unlikely it will ever return. Eliza is three months out."

"I know. That's why we're here, but like you said, we'll see what the labs say." *And what Jesus has to say.*

After passing some time waiting for the labs, our nurse jumped back into the room like a frog, beaming a smile and squatting down in delight. "Do you want to know what the labs are?"

Already fighting tears, I said, "Yes! Please!"

"I can't believe it! Eliza's creatinine is 1.1! That's normal, Shannon! I can't imagine she'll stay on dialysis!"

The shock and relief hit me all at once—I wasn't crazy! Jesus did move! Tears stung my eyes as I fell forward in my chair. "Thank You, Jesus. Thank You, thank You, Jesus."

A few minutes later, the doctor came in, mumbling to himself, "A miracle—there's no other explanation." We locked eyes, and I saw the shock and delight in his eyes. "Eliza will be going off dialysis today. With these numbers, there's no reason for her to be on it." The excitement was electric and rippled through the entire dialysis ward as my relief turned to laughter. *Oh, Lord, how can I thank You?*

My parents were the first people I longed to call as they had walked this long road by our sides, from the first all-night drive on September 11 to celebrating New Year's Day with us. Joel was driving the car as the other side of the line rang. *Come on, Dad, pick up!*

"Hey, what's up?"

"Dad, you sitting down? It's a miracle! Jesus moved, and Eliza is going off dialysis today! She's healed, Dad!"

The sound of choked-back tears could be heard on the other side of the line.

"Dad, you okay?"

The next several minutes were an accumulation of months of tears and emotion exploding into waves of pure joy. We cried, we laughed, and we praised the Lord together. What a moment of victory after a long season of battle!

> **Sent**: *Friday, January 12, 2007, 11:01a.m.*
> **Subject**: *Here's a math problem for you*
>
> *See the attached picture—it should bowl you over!*
> *I took it this morning after getting Eliza out of bed.*
> *Jesus is winking at us, as if to say, "See, I told you,*
> *I've always had really good things in store for you*
> *and Eliza!"*
>
> *Love,*
> *Shannon*

Eliza put her sister to shame today! This is after drinking 630ml of water all day yesterday!

Morning diaper comparison: Robin vs. Eliza

Sent: *Wednesday, January 17, 2007, 6:21 p.m.*
Subject: *Follow-up*

It's official, Eliza is doing great!! According to her blood draw on Monday, which I'm glad we braved the ice storm for, since Joel was able to stay home with the other two girls. I was picturing having to maneuver our double stroller through all this ice, and it was making my head spin! Eliza's creatinine was 1.3! She's doing awesome for being off dialysis for five days. The dialysis nurse told me that according to her lab information, for a child Eliza's age and weight, her creatinine should be somewhere between 0.5 and 1.2! That means Eliza was normal last week and is very close to normal now. Unfortunately, they didn't provide information on her phosphorus, so it's being retested. The only concern I had was the fact that her BUN went back up from 21 to 55. However, the doctor didn't seem surprised or bothered by it.

I spoke with Eliza's nutritionist this morning, and she has lifted all dietary restrictions but requested we increase her daily water intake. She said that her BUN could be high due to the amount of protein I'm giving her each day, which is funny, since high protein is a part of the renal diet. So I assume that since her kidneys are getting better, she needs to return to a more balanced diet. I have no problems with that! To celebrate, I gave her french fries with ketchup this afternoon for the first time, and she was in toddler heaven. She savored each bite.

We will need to have another blood draw in two weeks to make sure Eliza is continuing to maintain herself. The nurse mentioned that if problems are going to occur once you go off dialysis, they usually happen within the first two weeks. We are on week 1, with one to go—we were instructed to watch Eliza for any unusual behavior. I wanted to ask, "You mean beyond being two?" If she should start to sleep too much, throw up, pee less, or gain weight, it may be an indication that her creatinine has gone back up. Once we get to the two-week mark, we should just start coasting, as Eliza's creatinine level will start to plateau. If her labs look good in two weeks, they will wait another month before they recheck her. It may be two or three months before they remove her catheter tube—just as long as it happens before the pool opens! Eliza is our water baby, and I can't wait to take her swimming!

So just as quickly as all this happened, it vanishes. God is good! He has pulled us from the miry pit and set our feet on the rock of His grace and mercy! I believe in my heart that He has been telling me the past few days, "It is finished. What I set out to accomplish is complete."

Our home is full of joy and laughter again.
Thank you for walking next to us! We couldn't
have done this without the care and covering of so
many—Christ's church is an amazing thing!
Praise God, from whom all blessings flow!

In 2010, Eliza's healing was confirmed again by another nephrologist in Denver at Children's Hospital. We had moved to be near family, and I admit, it was really hard to adjust after all we had endured in Oklahoma.

The first appointment we had with our new nephrologist didn't happen quite as one would expect—he walked in the room quietly, looking at us with compassion, sat down with Eliza's medical file in his lap, and cleared his throat. "If I were to just look at Eliza on paper and nothing else, there's only one word for her: *miracle*." We spent the next hour sharing over tears the goodness of our Lord, both from the patient and doctor perspective. It was the most edifying and encouraging doctor's appointment I've ever had. He affirmed again that if—and he emphasized *if*—they ever see a patient's kidney function return as far out as Eliza's was, they always see it collapse again in a few days, as sometimes the kidneys have a final burst of function before collapsing. So he was blown away looking at her numbers—three years later, she was still maintaining a 0.9–1.2 creatinine!

This insight gave me pause as I reflected back on these two weeks after Eliza's kidney function returned. They were watching her very closely, but I wasn't entirely sure why. I knew there were risks, but not to this degree. I'm glad now that I didn't know the reality then, as it makes the freedom that much richer today. The Lord spared me from much unneeded stress.

On January 26, 2007, *The Oklahoman* newspaper ran another story on Eliza's miraculous healing. Our sweet friend and reporter came back to the house for another interview. It was scheduled to run on the front page of the local section. She had met with the editor the night before and been informed of its placement, even after advocating for it to be on the front page of the main section. The next day, when she entered work, people were congratulating her on another front-page story. "Yes, the front page of the local."

"What do you mean? No, it's on the front page in bold letters, 'Miraculous'!"

Entering the editor's office baffled, she looked to him for answers. "Don't ask me! I have no idea how it got there!"

The Lord did it—He put Himself on the front page of *The Oklahoman*! No one seemed to understand how it got there, but the response was amazing!

A big thank-you for renewing my attitude toward editing and what is newsworthy for the front page of our Oklahoma. During times like these (world of turmoil), we need to see on the front page some faith-based miracles. Again, my thanks to the editor and Lindsay!

This is wonderful and so awesome! God is truly good, and when people pray and believe, anything can happen!

I'm not sure how the staff at *The Oklahoman* ultimately felt about it, but it was sure a surprise to all of us. The Lord works in mysterious ways to accomplish His purposes.

Eliza holding The Oklahoman newspaper with the 'Miraculous' article

Aftermath

Sent: Wednesday, January 31, 2007, 9:26 p.m.
Subject: Lab work

I took Eliza in for lab work Monday morning, and the results and doctor's orders are finally available. Her creatinine is doing awesome—it's gone down to 1.1! Yes! Her phosphorus is normal, which is great! Apparently, the doctor said it's time to make arrangements to have Eliza's dialysis catheter tube removed! I'm still reeling over this, wondering, Is it too soon? We've been told it could be a few months before they consider taking it out, and now we're talking about removing it already? Wow! The nurse said that realistically, it could still be a month or so, depending on the surgery schedule. We should have a date next week. Crazy, crazy, crazy.

Sent: Tuesday, February 27, 2007, 5:51 p.m.
Subject: I bet you're wondering

It's been a month since I sent out an update, and I'm sorry I haven't responded to many of your inquiries! Eliza is doing well. We still have some work ahead of us, but it's easy, way easy in comparison to where we should be or would be without Jesus's intervention.

Eliza has met with a speech therapist once a week over the past month, which has really helped her blossom in many respects. Eliza went three months without using her mouth for anything but grunting, which set her back a bit. I had no idea how important it is for one- to two-year-olds to be using their mouths for eating, putting things in their mouths, etc., which helps them develop their language skills. So, moms, let your kids chew on their toes and lick lemons—it's really good for them!

The speech therapist has noticed two things: One, Eliza is doing incredibly well with her fine motor skills, given what she endured. She initially thought based on Eliza's MRI and paperwork that she'd have to focus more on general coordination skills, but Eliza is excelling in that area. Yes!

However, the second thing the therapist noticed is that Eliza still seems to have a "disconnect" in her brain, which is often seen in stroke victims. When you sit down to read a book with Eliza, you can point at an object and have her repeat the word to you five to six times without any problems, but once you ask her, "What is that, Eliza?" she'll look at you as if you're from Mars even though she has just repeated the word to you several times. She's an excellent repeater, but a poor reporter. Even though she's said the word, her brain isn't quite registering the word. But even with the challenge, her vocabulary has doubled this month, so I'm sure that with continued therapy and practice, her brain will "reconnect" itself.

I'm taking Eliza in to see her nephrologist tomorrow morning for more lab work, and I'm hoping and praying they will set a surgery date to have the catheter tube removed. It has been a frustrating month as we're realizing how little communication our doctors (nephrologists) have among themselves. Our doctor last month said it was time to go ahead and set a surgery date, but then he rotated out of the clinic, and doctor number 2 stepped in. Doctor 2 wasn't sure it was time to take the tube out and requested we make an appointment for him to see Eliza, which meant we had to wait until the last day in February to get in. My main concern: Thursday, March 1, doctor number 3 rotates into the clinic, and she may have some of her own concerns and thought to throw into the mix, which may mean waiting again.

The nurses have appeared confused and unsure what steps need to be taken in regards to Eliza's care, so we've just sat around all month, waiting as patiently as possible for tomorrow, continuing to give Eliza her prescribed calcium carbonate with each meal and iron twice a day, wondering if she still needs them. So I'm very hopeful our appointment tomorrow will be productive and conclusive. But to the doctor's credit, Children's Hospital did just move into the newly remodeled tower across the street, which I'm sure has created confusion.

Eliza's lab work tomorrow will give us insight into the condition of her kidneys—it's been long enough now that they should have leveled off in their healing process. Whatever we see tomorrow is likely indicative of what she will continue to have as she grows. If her creatinine is still in the 1 range, then she has incurred some long-term damage—not enough to require dialysis or transplant, but potentially enough to keep an eye on. I'm really praying her BUN has gone down again. Her BUN is the by-product of water from ingesting protein. We've tried to monitor how much protein she's eating without cutting it out altogether, as she needs it to grow! I realized, though, that right before her last lab work, I had been feeding her a lot of cottage cheese, which is packed full of protein. I can't help but wonder if that contributed to the higher BUN number of 51 (18–20 normal).

The nephrologist told me that the creatinine and BUN are often in correlation with each other. So if her creatinine is not normal, her BUN is not going to be normal either, since they both have to do with waste cycled through the kidneys.

Some of you have asked how we're doing as a family: Have we adjusted back to normal life? I suppose so. Joel is crazy with work and trying to balance between home and his busy patient load. I'm still having a hard time getting library books back on time, but the girls are thrilled we're going to the library again. The dialysis machine in Eliza's room is quickly becoming a faded memory, other than the staining on their bedroom carpet from the Nepro and dialysis solution. It sits neglected and covered with a cardboard box. Baxter is supposed to come pick it up at some point, but we haven't heard anything. Life is moving on.

Spring has come!

Sent: *Thursday, March 1, 2007, 4:27 p.m.*
Subject: *Eliza's appointment*

I finally got Eliza's lab results back from yesterday. I'm very happy to report that her body is maintaining itself just fine without dialysis! Her creatinine went down again to 1.0 (it was 1.1 last month, 0.4–0.7 normal), and her BUN has gone down to 40 (7–18 normal)—she was 51 last month. Her phosphorus is perfectly normal! The doctor has decided to keep things just as they are. We are to continue giving her calcium carbonate with each meal (which helps bind with her phosphorus to keep that number down) and iron twice a day.

But here's the great news: Eliza is scheduled for surgery to have her catheter tube removed next Tuesday! I wasn't expecting it to happen that quickly—I thought the end of March would be the earliest possibility. It should be a quick outpatient procedure, not requiring a hospital stay. I think we've spent enough time there this past year that I will gladly bring Eliza home. I don't have a surgery time yet. I'm supposed to call a lady in surgery Monday morning to get the details. I get the impression that if things are crazy or too many emergencies arise, we may be rescheduled. I'm fine with that too, since we know what it's like having to wait for surgery, especially when you feel like your child's life is on the line. Children's operating rooms have doubled in their new building, so hopefully that will no longer be an issue.

Eliza's long-term prognosis: not sure. We are to continue follow-up appointments each month at the dialysis unit. This is actually a step in the right direction, since she's no longer on dialysis; we no longer have to go to the dialysis clinic. Each time we've visited the clinic, there have been several babies and young children connected to hemodialysis, which is hard to see. I remain forever thankful the Lord saved Eliza from having to endure hemo— peritoneal dialysis from home was much easier for her body than hemo would have been.

The doctor determined that they would continue to check Eliza once a month for a while until they're certain her body is maintaining itself, then we may eventually taper off our visits to every three months, six months, yearly, etc. At the end of March, they may run a test to see how well Eliza's kidneys are handling her BUN. They will test her urine to see if it has large amounts of protein in it. If it does, then it means her kidneys are not filtering her protein back into her bloodstream. Typically, you don't just pee out the protein you ingest; it gets cycled through your kidneys back into your bloodstream. There is a medication they can prescribe that would help the healthy nephrons in Eliza's kidneys cycle the protein more efficiently. The healthy nephrons are working overtime right now to make up for the damaged ones, which could be causing the increased BUN. The medicine would help calm everything down and make the healthy nephrons more efficient. I'm not sure why they don't just prescribe that now, but I suppose they want to give her a little more time to see if her body will continue to recover on its own. No need for extra medication, right?

Eliza's speech therapist and I were both surprised this morning by the progress she seems to have made in just this past week. Eliza was pointing to objects around the room, trying to say the words; they don't sound right, but this is the first time I've seen her attempt to say things she's not comfortable with or doesn't know how to pronounce. Lindy and I just sat there looking at each other in mock surprise. Did she just say that? This little fighter is going to be just fine.

Our sweet speech therapist, Lindy, didn't confide in me until much later how concerned she was for Eliza during our first visit. Since Eliza was showing signs of a stroke victim, only able to parrot words back but unable to assimilate them in her mind, we were looking at a long road of therapy to gain healing. But amazingly, over the span of two months, Lindy and I (unknowingly) watched another miracle unfold before us as Eliza's ability to use language kicked into gear. Instead of needing months, if not years, of therapy, Eliza's brain recov-

ered within the few months of Lindy's care. The Lord was continuing what He had begun in Eliza.

*****

Sent: *Monday, March 5, 2007, 9:15 p.m.*
Subject: *Surgery confirmed*

At ten thirty tomorrow morning, Eliza will be going in for surgery. The procedure only takes about forty-five minutes to an hour, and then we will stay at Children's for another hour or two, depending on how she's doing postop. I will be taking Eliza in alone; Joel is slammed and unable to take the day off, but I know his heart will not be far. Plus, we don't go to Children's anymore without seeing someone we know, so I'm sure I'll end up occupied one way or another.

I've tried to tell Eliza it's time to say goodbye to the tube, but I don't think she gets it. It's like trying to tell a toddler to say goodbye to their arm—it has no meaning to them other than, "Yes, I have an arm. Want to see it?" Over the past six months, the tube has become just another part of her body, which she often reminds me of. Did I pin it on her shirt right, change the bandage, etc.? She's kind of finicky and somewhat attached.

Zoë and Robin are spending tomorrow night with friends. They were all a-twitter this evening as I packed their overnight bag to stay with friends, until Robin looked at me seriously. "Iza?"

"No, Mommy is taking Eliza to the hospital." Her face dropped, and I thought she might cry. "No, Robin, it's okay. She's coming home right away." I don't know if she understands or not, but apparently, she does know what it means to have Eliza

in the "hospital." Pray for her dear heart tomorrow as I drop them off at their friend's house and Eliza remains in the car. Ah, twins—they are special. Robin is so tender with Eliza, rubbing her head as I change her catheter dressing each night. "It's okay, Iza."

This feels like the final chapter of our six-month journey. Lord willing, tomorrow or Wednesday will be my final update on Eliza! Imagine, an inbox without messages from Shannon, other than nice, social ones! How grand!

I truly thank God every time I remember you! My dream team!

*****

Sent*: Tuesday, March 6, 2007, 9:02 p.m.*
Subject*: Home resting*

Eliza is doing great—home resting after a long morning.

We arrived at the hospital on time around 8:00 a.m. for registration after dropping the girls off. Eliza cried as Robin and Zoë left. She really wanted to go play! After registration, we sat around in a very packed operating registration room, wondering what each child could possibly need surgically. Most of them looked as healthy as Eliza! At 9:15 a.m., they pulled us back to an exam room to prepare Eliza for anesthesia and more paperwork. Unfortunately, she was running a fever of 100.4! I had no idea she had a fever! She had a cold last week but has seemed fine the past two days. The nurse went to speak with the surgeon and anesthetic doctor for direction. Typically, they would not perform surgery on anyone with a fever due to the risk of increased infection. But because the removal of the tube is a very simple procedure that only requires gas to knock her out, they decided to proceed. I was very thankful for this news since the outer cap on her dialysis tube came off somehow while I was changing her into the yellow hospital pajamas. If they didn't proceed, I was going to have to take Eliza upstairs to the dialysis unit anyway to change out that part of her tube, which would have meant more antibiotics to stop any infection. An open tube is a direct airway into her peritoneal cavity. Crazy! That's the first time (and last) the cap has come off!

I was only in the operating waiting room long enough to call a few family members when the surgeon called my name. The procedure was already done? And it only took twenty minutes from the time they wheeled Eliza away! The surgeon explained that, really, all they do is yank the tube out with their hands. I was shocked! That's it? I'm glad I didn't know that beforehand—the thought of someone pulling that hard on my daughter is horrible, at least to a mom. It would be like someone supergluing a tube to their belly button and then having someone pull on it until it popped off—ouch!

The surgeon mentioned that as they pulled out the tube, some yellow gunk came to the surface, which may be a sign of an infection. I can't help but wonder if that explains her fever. There is a round sponge that has been left in Eliza for the original surgery that should dissolve over time (at least I hope it dissolves). However, if she does have an infection inside her peritoneum, it could attach to the sponge, which may require taking the sponge out surgically. So they are culturing the yellow substance at the end of her tube for infection. They will first treat it with antibiotics, but if her original scar (which has healed already) turns red, or if her fever persists, she may require further attention. Bummer.

Within thirty minutes of speaking with the surgeon, I was called back to see Eliza. She looked great! Tired, but great! We were discharged without any complications, and I brought her home. Sadly, she tossed her cookies (or graham crackers) all over the back seat within minutes of home. Apparently, she wasn't handling the aftereffects of the anesthesia as well as I thought. So I cleaned up, Lord willing, my last bout of throw-up regarding Eliza's illness. She cheerfully sat on the driveway, watching me clean up everything. When I changed her into new clothes, she said, "Pin, oh no!" She was looking for her tube to pin to the inside of her shirt. She kept saying, "Oh no! Oh no!"

All in all, today was a success!

Sent: *Friday, March 16, 2007, 9:27 p.m.*
Subject: *Freedom!*

The girls and I just returned from donating twenty-six boxes of dialysis supplies weighing a total of 615 pounds!! I packed every crook and cranny of our Honda car to deliver it in one trip. With boxes stacked on the floor, the girls' feet were practically touching the car ceiling! What a sight we were. I hardly recognized the girls' empty closet—I could practically swim in there with all the reclaimed space!

Eliza enjoyed her first bath this week in six months. She was in heaven! She splashed and giggled so much I was afraid we'd have to pry her out of the tub, but once she was good and pickled, she decided enough was enough. We've taken her Band-Aid off her exit site, and it looks fantastic! The hole has filled in beautifully, and Eliza is adjusting to the feeling of free skin. She still enjoys lifting her shirt to show off her wound to anyone who appears moderately interested, even the postal lady and grocery store clerk! I guess when you're as cute as she is, you can get away with just about anything.

The Lord brought a passage of Scripture to mind this past weekend. He reminded me of John 6:53–67, when Jesus said, "'I tell you the truth, unless you eat the flesh of the Son of Man and drink His blood, you have no life in you.' On hearing it, many of His disciples said, 'This is a hard teaching. Who can accept it?' From this time many of His disciples turned back and no longer followed Him. 'You do not want to leave too, do you?' Jesus asked the twelve."

There are going to be times in our lives when God asks us the same question. The Lord may ask us to face circumstances that have caused others to stop following Jesus or led them into bitterness toward Him. A time may come when Jesus's teaching, timing, or leading may seem hard to understand. It's in these times that Jesus asks us, "You do not want to leave me too, do you?"

Jesus is such a gentleman. He won't barge His way into a place He's not welcome. We all have the choice of walking away, grumbling, turning to bitterness, or choosing our own path. It's our right— the right God has given each one of us—choice. But as believers who know the Lord, such as the twelve, He's going to ask, "You don't want to leave me too, do you?" It's my prayer that we all respond the same way Simon Peter did in verse 68, "Lord, to whom shall we go? You have the words of eternal life. We believe that You are the Holy One of God." Amen!

We have the ability now to look back on these teachings of Jesus and recognize communion, but the twelve were confounded as to what God meant. They had to follow Jesus by faith, trusting His words to be true, good, and intentional, even though they appeared out of character.

So it is with our lives; things are not always going to look good or make any sense, but once we get through on faith, we will have the ability to look back with hindsight to see what was true, good, and intentional.

I want to encourage you to run; keep running and don't stop running until you've reached the end. We need to finish strong in the Lord. Our finish is just as important as our beginning. In a race, it's the runners who have endured and trained to cross the finish line. Many, many runners will step up to the starting block, eager to finish, but only a few will reach the end. We are running a dangerous race sprinkled with roadblocks, but, brothers and sisters, keep running! Finish well! There will be rest on the other side of the line; it's a promise to those of us who believe!

Epilogue

Since the writing of this book, our family's story has continued to twist and turn in the most unexpected ways, with multiple moves to five different states, job changes, new illnesses, including a rare form of epilepsy for Robin (another miraculous moment), and unemployment. But through it all, the Lord's sovereignty has continued to astound us, as His story for our life has always been better than how we would write our own. Eliza, now in her teen years, has grown into a beautiful young woman with a quiet trust in her Savior. Her kidneys continue to hold their own, maintaining the same 40 to 50 percent function. However, transplant is never completely out of our vocabulary, as we know the day might come when the Lord says, "It's time." Months after the Lord moved on Eliza, I lamented, "Lord, why wasn't the healing 100 precent? All the healings we read about in Scripture appear complete. Why not hers?" I really wrestled with these questions until the Lord gently reminded me, "Do you remember what you had prayed for Eliza?"

"Ah, yes. Right, Lord. I asked repeatedly that her life would not be dependent on anything other than You." I didn't want her life dependent on a machine, medications, or doctors. I wanted her life completely dependent on Him and Him alone. And you know what? That is exactly where we have lived these many years since. We trust the one who said, "It is finished." He accomplished what He desired then, and I know He will continue to walk with Eliza regardless of the physical outcome—He is unable to be anything other than good. Why would we not continue to trust Him?

Discussion Questions

Chapter 1

1. When Joel says in his prayer, "Help us to give Eliza back to You, she is really Yours and Yours alone, she doesn't belong to us," what do you think he meant by that? Is there someone in your life you need to give back to the Lord?
2. What do you think Job 1:20–21 means? "At this, Job got up and tore his robe and shaved his head. Then he fell to the ground in worship and said: 'Naked I came from my mother's womb, and naked I will depart. The Lord gave and the Lord has taken away; may the name of the Lord be praised.'"

Chapter 2

1. What does it mean to willingly enter God's rest?
2. What does Jesus pray for Simon in Luke 22:31? Why do you think our faith is important to God?
3. What was Job's first response to suffering in Job 1:20?
4. What is your initial response to trials?

Chapter 4

1. According to Psalm 63:3–5, what does David consider better than life?
2. Where was David when he wrote this Psalm? Hint: see verse 1.
3. Why do you think that could be significant?

Chapter 5

1. According to 2 Corinthians 4:16–18, why do we not lose heart? What are we to fix our eyes on?
2. What does it mean to be "poor in spirit," as found in Matthew 5:3?
3. What question does Job challenge us with in Job 2:10?
4. According to Isaiah 29:13, what were the Israelites doing? Is it possible to love the Lord with your lips but not your heart?
5. What does God admonish the Israelites for doing in Isaiah 28:10–13? How do you see this happening today?
6. What does God do in Matthew 5:45b? Why do you think this is significant?

Chapter 7

1. In what way did Shannon feel like she had fellowshipped with Eve?
2. What do you think Proverbs 26:11 means?

Chapter 8

1. In what ways do we look to other people to determine our walk with the Lord?
2. Are there things in your life that the Lord needs to uproot?
3. How did Jesus challenge the disciples in John 6:52–71? What was their response to Him?
4. Have you ever been tempted to walk away from the Lord because you didn't understand what He was doing? How do these verses encourage your heart?

Chapter 10

1. Read 1 Corinthians 1:25, 27–19. In what ways does God use the weak things of this world?

2. According to Hebrews 3:7–14, how do we come to share in Jesus? What is our confidence? And what is Jesus warning us against?
3. Why are we to encourage one another according to Hebrews 3:12?
4. What does the word *harden* mean in Hebrews 3:8? What is the best way to determine the true state of our hearts?
5. Which did Joel and Shannon choose to put their faith in, God doing this or that or in *who* God is, His character?

Chapter 11

1. What does Hebrews 5:7–9 tell us about Jesus? Does this surprise you? Why?
2. Why do you think people run from suffering when it holds such rich hope of knowing Jesus better?
3. According to Hebrews 4:16, what can we receive from the Lord?
4. What is the difference between grace and mercy?
5. According to Oswald Chambers, what is the point of prayer?

Chapter 12

1. What is unique about the Canaanite woman's interaction with Jesus in Matthew 15:21–28?
2. How does Jesus respond to her?
3. What is considered of great value in 1 Peter 1:6–9?
4. Where was Jesus during the storm in Matthew 6:45–52? Were the disciples ever outside His reach?
5. Do you look for Jesus in the midst of your storms, or are you too busy straining at the oars, believing your survival will come from our own strength to endure?

Chapter 13

1. What is the will of God according to Philippians 4:4? Is there a difference between rejoicing in the Lord and rejoicing in your circumstances?
2. In Romans 8:28, we were promised that God will work all things for our good, but according to Romans 8:29, what is the ultimate good promised to the believer?
3. According to Romans 1:20–22, where does backsliding in the life of a believer begin?

Chapter 15

1. What do you think Shannon meant when she said, "It is my prayer that I would forever carry the mark of the lion"?

Chapter 16

1. What does *Emmanuel* mean? Does it have any significance in your own life? Why or why not?
2. According to Philippians 2:6–8, what did Jesus do? Why was it significant?

About the Author

Shannon Schulz puts her trust in Jesus Christ and loves bringing Scripture to life for others. She is a Bible teacher for women's groups and homeschool co-ops, sharing her story as often as possible. Shannon is married to her best friend, Joel, and together they live in Oklahoma with their three daughters, Zoë, Eliza, and Robin. She can be reached through her website: www.splitseas.com